Conversation M

Conversation Matters

How to Engage Effectively with One Another

Peter Shaw CB

continuum
LONDON • NEW YORK

Continuum

The Tower Building
11 York Road
London SE1 7NX

15 East 26th Street
Suite 1703
New York, NY 10010

www.continuumbooks.com

First published 2005

British Library Cataloguing-in-Publication Data
A catalogue record for this book is available from the British
Library.

ISBN 0 8264 8147 7

Typeset by YHT Ltd, London
Printed and bound by MPG Books Ltd, Bodmin, Cornwall

In memory of my parents who set me on my way

Frank Shaw	1895–1956
Ursula Lister Shaw	1913–1998

Contents

Foreword

'The greatest tool we have at our disposal is the power of conversation.' A bold claim, but one which Peter Shaw amply justifies in this compelling book. All our lives are enriched and shaped by conversations. This week mine have included a brief but significant exchange with a vicar 12 hours before she died of cancer – brief because her strength could not sustain more; significant because we both knew it was probably a farewell (and we parted in a mutual prayer for blessing), and also because we needed to resolve a decision which could deeply affect another person's ministry. I have also shared in discussions this week with colleagues which could shape the diocese over the next five years, and had the rich enjoyment of conversations over the dinner table with all the ordinands in the diocese.

These verbal exchanges have the potential to instruct us, bring us a range of emotions from deep sadness to laughter and great joy, deepen our relationships and launch initiatives and ideas. Conversation is indeed a powerful tool. Its power and effectiveness is well illustrated in the life of Jesus Christ, from his childhood discussions with the teachers in the temple (which caused his mother much anxiety) to his brief but effective act of concern for Mary as she stood weeping at the foot of the cross with John the disciple, 'Dear woman, here is your son', and the fascinating conversation with Cleopas and his companion on the way to Emmaus. Wouldn't we just love to listen in?

The desire to communicate is compelling, as the thousands of text messages which criss-cross the globe testify. But these brief and truncated messages, pared to the impersonal minimum, carry the danger of undermining the value of face-to-face conversation. Real conversation is an art to be developed and enjoyed.

Taking examples from the relationships between Jesus and a number of different individuals, Peter draws on his own experience of conversation to help us make the opportunity to communicate more effective and enjoyable. He explores seven different types of conversation (listening, encouraging, challenging, short, painful, unresponsive and joyful). In each case he invites us to consider examples of the way Jesus used conversations to achieve the desired outcome, and helps us to reflect on the way we could do the same. Just as Jesus focused on engagement, discernment and stretching his hearers, so we can make our communication do the same.

The result is a book which will repay careful reflection by both individuals and groups. Its seven central chapters could well form the basis of a Lenten study. I have thoroughly enjoyed reading it and have been not only entertained and encouraged but also provoked into thinking how I could use the practical advice and questions for reflection which conclude each chapter. Like all tools, our conversation can be sharpened and polished, for sparkling conversation is a delight to be enjoyed.

Peter Shaw is well qualified to be our guide through this most enriching of subjects. With a distinguished career in the civil service, experience in coaching leaders and as a reader in the Church of England, he is well versed in the variety and power of different conversations. Conversations with Peter have always been enjoyable and instructive. While Sydney Smith could say of Macaulay that 'he has occasional flashes of silence that make his conversation delightful', it has been the flashes of inspiration and insight that make Peter's memorable for me. Though silence, of course, is its own conversation, as Peter tellingly reminds us in quoting Mother Teresa on prayer.

+Ian Cundy, Bishop of Peterborough

Introduction

The quality of conversation matters for healthy family life, community life and work life. This book aims to revitalize conversation as an important means of communication. Its goal is to help you enjoy conversation as a medium to learn and as a means of influencing others. My hope is that you are excited by the opportunity conversation offers to understand and encourage, and stimulated to be fully part of a wider range of conversations.

Conversation is crucial to the way we enjoy our days and grow in understanding. This introduction is written at the end of a week walking in Swaledale. We have had friendly conversations with farmers, walkers, shopkeepers and publicans. We met old friends for dinner and talked deeply about work priorities. We went to an inaugural lecture at Durham University and discussed challenging issues. We talked with students over coffee about their hopes for the future. When our children arrived from London, there was much fun and laughter in the conversations. Yesterday we went to a wedding where there were joyful conversations with old and new friends, including a school friend I had not seen for nearly 40 years. Each conversation was different and special.

We can all look back to role models who have influenced the way we use the power of conversation. Jesus is an excellent starting point as he used conversation in a wide range of ways. He engaged through listening, he discerned through his questioning, and he stretched through focusing on key issues and challenging people to reach conclusions.

George, a colleague, takes part each year in the Wintershall Passion Play, an annual event in the Surrey Hills which enacts the life of Jesus. For a number of years George was one of the disciples. He tells me that he became completely absorbed in the part. It was as if the actors were with Jesus himself. The conversations with Jesus felt alive. In every performance, when it came to the crucifixion George felt mortified and near to tears. Enacting these conversations stretched his thinking. It was as if he was near Jesus himself and not only near to an actor playing the part of Jesus.

My passion for developing our skills in conversation results from thoroughly enjoying my second career as an executive coach. It is my joy to give people space to talk. In these very informal conversations listening to understand is crucial. I must allow people to work through difficult subjects. People must always go out of the discussions encouraged. Sometimes there are moments of pure joy. The power of conversation is more than the words. It is the engagement of two people bringing understanding and then stretching that understanding.

Conversations come in many different shapes and sizes. Every one is different. I have focused on seven different types of conversations, namely listening, encouraging, challenging, short, painful, unresponsive and joyful. Each one has its own dynamics and brings different emotions. At the start of each chapter are two examples of conversations in which Jesus engaged, followed by examples of relevant contemporary conversations, practical ideas with themes and questions to reflect on individually or in groups. My aim is to be practical.

There are many people who have influenced me in

Introduction

formulating the contents of this book. Of special importance have been my excellent colleagues at Praesta Partners, Chris Jagger and other members of Busbridge Parish
Church, who have heard some of this material in a series
of talks and given me valuable reflections, Lesley Mason,
Ruth Bennett and Linda Brown, who commented so
thoroughly on an early draft, the Continuum editor
Carolyn Armitage, who has been a great source of practical wisdom, and Judy Smith, who has been a superb
typist. Thanks especially to Frances and our children
Graham, Ruth and Colin for their willingness to put up
with my disappearing into the study.

So enjoy the book, and the many conversations that
follow.

Peter Shaw
May 2005
Swaledale

Conversations that engage, discern and stretch 1

Dawn and Mark are two of the people at the end of the telephone when you phone 999 in Scotland and ask for an ambulance. They are highly skilled in the art of conversation in a very focused way. Their job is to extract key information from each caller as quickly as possible to enable the ambulance to be dispatched. They are often talking to people gripped with fear. They want to be sympathetic, but the most crucial task is to get the ambulance to the scene of the accident as fast as possible.

Often it is difficult for Dawn and Mark to extract the right information. The caller will shout, 'I'm in the High Street!' without saying which high street. Sometimes the callers are panicking or screaming. Often they are not really listening. The panic has blocked their ears to the steady advice of Dawn and Mark.

Dawn and Mark cope with each individual's fear through their calm and measured approach. Each call is different. When they are on the phone they have no one to turn to. They talk of painful conversations when there are cot deaths: there is nothing they can do on the end of a phone that can help. Sometimes the most acute distress is not with the severest of problems. A mother cries bitterly that she has trapped the fingers of her 4-year-old in the door: it is not life threatening but is still emotionally painful. There are joyful moments in helping a mother through childbirth. Mark told me of one occasion when, following his advice on mouth-to-mouth resuscitation, someone began breathing again.

In a 12-hour shift Dawn and Mark will have about 150 conversations. Dawn has had one letter of thanks in two years, but that limited sense of gratitude does not detract from the pleasure of doing the job. Often people just hang up the phone without saying 'Thank you', when the ambulance arrives. The mix of painful and joyful conversations is part of the job. I was struck by their calmness and ability to cope so well with the fear in others. They taught me much about the power of conversation that is focused and adaptable.

The greatest tool we have at our disposal is the power of conversation. We so easily underestimate its significance. The power is not only in the words. It is created by the engagement and the emotional reactions between two people. When words are used unkindly and without thought, they have the potential to do huge damage. But conversation also has the potential to uplift, to enliven and to encourage. Through a conversation we learn more about ourselves as well as others. Through the richness of conversation we move out of ourselves and engage with others so that our hopes and thoughts are shared and developed.

At the heart of conversation is good listening. Dawn and Mark have to listen so carefully to what each 999 caller is saying. Martin Luther King talked of the deep suffering caused by being deprived of a listening ear: 'When I am not listened to, I feel hurt, angry, destroyed, lonely.' In his book *Long Walk to Freedom*, Nelson Mandela emphasized that he always endeavoured to listen to what each person wanted to say before venturing his own opinion.

The Oxford English Dictionary has a number of definitions of the word 'conversation'. The most easily recognized definition is 'the interchange of thought and words'. Other definitions give us different dimensions of conversation. Definitions such as 'the action of living or having one's being in or among' and 'the action of consorting with others, living together' bring out the dimension of conversation which is not just about words but includes an intimacy of thought and action. The richness of the word 'conversation' flows from its relevance at so many different levels of human engagement. It embraces conversations within a family, within a community, within a society and within the work environment.

Conversation can grow in unexpected ways. When I was doing jury service recently there was a shared sense of humour that developed between the group of fellow jurors. Having to reach a unanimous view reinforced the quality of conversation between us.

Conversations go through many different phases. As a postgraduate student I shared a house with a good friend. As we went on long walks in the Pennines or sat in the pub, we talked of our hopes and fears in many aspects of our lives. Thirty-five years later the friendship is as strong, but my friend has become very disabled and the conversation is conducted through his eyes, the occasional word, the raising of a hand or a nod. Words are limited, but there is a depth of memories which helps ensure a quality of conversation that still holds true. It is an important reminder to cherish and enjoy each conversation whatever the circumstances.

Starting points

Jesus is an excellent starting point when we come to look at the power of conversation. Jesus communicated through the spoken word and not the written word. The Gospel stories are full of conversations that Jesus had. It was through conversations that he shared his teaching. It was as people talked with him that they either embraced his message or moved some distance from it. But how did Jesus manage to use conversation as such an effective tool? He dared to use conversation in a variety of powerful ways. He was engaged, discerning and stretching in the way he related to his friends, his supporters and his critics.

Jesus *engaged* through listening, building trust, talking with people directly and showing a strong level of empathy with those people. He *showed discernment* through his questioning, his clarity, his curiosity and the flexibility with which he used different approaches in talking with different people. He *stretched* through focusing on key issues, debating, challenging and pushing people to reach conclusions. There was a combination of focus and freedom in all his conversations.

Jesus grew up in a world where the passing on of stories from one generation to another was crucial to the Jewish tradition. The transmission of stories through conversation was a very powerful means of embedding the cultural heritage in the thinking of the next generation. This is perhaps best summed up in the tradition of the Passover Supper, when the story of the deliverance of the Children of Israel would be recounted through each generation.

The Old Testament Scriptures capture the best of traditional wisdom passed on through conversation. They are full of stories of conversations between the prophets and God. History and wise teachings were communicated through accounts of conversations between Samuel and God about who should be king, between Moses and God about his leadership, and between Job and God about coping with suffering. Proverbs is full of thoughtful words about conversation: 'He who holds his tongue is wise' (10.19), and 'The tongue that brings healing is a tree of life, but a deceitful tongue crushes the spirit' (15.4).

The themes of engagement, discernment and stretching are evident in the writing of the first apostles. In his letter to the Colossians Paul ends with a series of exhortations about being watchful and thankful, being wise in the way you act towards outsiders and making the most of every opportunity. He urges his readers, 'Let your conversation be always full of grace, seasoned with salt, so that you may know how to answer everyone' (4.6).

The epistle written by James is full of practical good sense. He says, 'Be quick to listen, slow to speak and slow to become angry' (1.19). Chapter 3 is all about taming the tongue. He describes the tongue as 'a small part of the body, but it makes great boasts' (3.5). He caricatures the tongue as a fire which can corrupt the whole person. He contrasts the reality that, 'With the tongue we praise our Lord and Father, and with it we curse men, who have been made in God's likeness' (3.9). Before leading into a section on wisdom James says, 'Out of the same mouth come praise and cursing. My brothers, this should not be' (3.10). James focuses on the 'deeds done in the humility that comes from wisdom' (3.13). For him this is the wisdom that 'is first of all pure; then peace-loving, considerate, submissive, full of mercy and good fruit, impartial and sincere' (3.17). He sets together the wise use of the tongue and this quality of wisdom: the wise use of the tongue which brings wisdom, engages, discerns and stretches.

The second starting point is the changing nature of conversations within our day-to-day worlds. Leaders in many organizations are increasingly expected to be visible, and this has put a much greater emphasis on the spoken word. The expectation is that leaders will communicate not just through written messages but through talking at open meetings, being interviewed and entering into direct discussion with staff. This focus on conversation is at the centre of good communication within thriving business organizations.

The same process is apparent within the voluntary sector and the churches. No longer will people accept orders from someone standing six feet above contradiction. Any change in church life or in the running of a charity needs to include effective consultation and conversation so that the participants are fully engaged and energized to move on to new things.

This focus on the power of conversation is evidenced in particular through the growth of coaching and mentoring within virtually every sector. One-to-one conversation is increasingly seen as a powerful means of developing understanding and clarifying next steps. These conversations are about creating a safe environment in which individuals can talk through their hopes and fears and reach conclusions that often go beyond their thinking prior to the start of the conversation. Coaches or mentors are aiming to help those individuals fully embrace their strengths and work through what they find most demanding. Exploring difficult issues might involve rehearsing different approaches, experimenting with those approaches, and then talking through what has or has not worked. Many people find they know what they think when they hear themselves say it. Hence the value in these one-to-one conversations lies in enabling individuals to clarify their way forward.

A third starting point is technology. Our means of communication are changing dramatically in our families, communities, churches and work environments. Videos, DVDs and the wider range of TV channels provide us with a wealth of information. We communicate faster and faster through emailing and texting. Texting is a superb way of communicating a brief thought or fact. The mobile phone has saved people from many hours waiting patiently at railway stations for delayed trains.

This wonderful technology, however, is not enough on its own. Emailing is a great way of conveying information quickly, but working through to a solution often needs the human interaction that only talking together can provide. Emailing can be a very sterile way of trying to solve a problem. The subtlety of conversation needs to be added to the clarity of the text message if a relationship is to grow. It is not a question of emailing *or* conversation, but rather emailing *and* conversation. People talking, sharing and laughing together is an essential part of making communication work in a way that fully embraces each person.

Your most significant conversations

Conversations are not about what other people do. Each day we all engage in conversation. All conversations have a value, but some are more helpful than others. Some are very positive, while others can be damaging. Conversations occur from an early age when words are primitive. The first communication with a tiny baby is through sharing a smile. Conversation at the other end of the age spectrum may well be confused and sometimes clouded with memory loss. Stories are often repeated many times, but still have a crucial part to play in an individual's identity.

How important have significant conversations been in your life? Can you reflect on the most significant conversations for you? For me the most significant conversations were these:

- Sitting on my mother's knee aged 7 talking about my father who had just died.
- Standing outside a tent at a Crusader camp for young people talking with one of the leaders about embracing the Christian faith in a more explicit way than I had done before.
- Being challenged by a former boss to be willing to be more stretched and less captive to my background.
- Casual conversations over the washing-up which have turned into special memories because of the humour or shared stories.
- Various conversations with Frances when we were going out together about the possibility of marriage.
- Conversations with my mother during her final years when her memory was less good but the conversations were especially important.
- Conversations with our children at critical stages in their lives, when I may not always have been entirely helpful.
- Conversations with my eldest son about 'imagining' I was 21 again at the time when it was right to move on from my career in government.

- Conversations with people I have coached who went out from these discussions with a more positive frame of mind than when we began.

These conversations were all very important to me. You will have parallel instances covering personal, family and work issues where conversation has been both important to you and it has been a privilege to share in a friend's life and experience.

I am sure it helps to look at conversations across the whole of our lives and not to compartmentalize them into specifically personal, family or professional. Conversations are so powerful at transition points in our lives, when we are deliberately looking across boundaries at the interaction between personal, family and work issues. Sometimes our conversations need to flow across these boundaries in order to bring insight from one world into another. When we face pressures in our work environment or in our community or church worlds, often the soundest advice and the best conversations are with someone who has some sensitivity to our world but is actually operating in a different arena. Such conversations often bring reality, objectivity and good sense.

Patterns in conversations

Have you observed certain patterns in conversations? Do you recognize any of the following?

- Have you shared in the intensity of a conversation with a child who is full of excitement about new things? The conversation bounces around with lots of life and fantasy; you feel uplifted by the pleasure of that conversation.

- Have you observed how children aged 12 have fairly one-dimensional conversations with each other about football or schoolwork, but at 15 they begin to have long, detailed conversations about everything under the sun? What a delight to see that transition into young people enjoying their peer group and talking enthusiastically about anything and everything.

- Have you observed friendships where the contribution to conversation is a 50:50 split, then gradually the friendship begins to die as the balance becomes 80:20 and then 90:10? What sadness to see a friendship based on quality conversation gradually losing its energy and power.

- Have you been saddened by spending time with an older person who has virtually stopped talking? This is a tragic loss of human interaction, when someone – through physical or mental incapacity – has lost the will or power to share in conversation. The words we use can still be a powerful force for good, even if it is just the eyes that are showing some response and not the mouth.

- Have you shared in conversations with individuals where the gap of a couple of years is as a second? You pick up in conversation exactly where you left off years ago and feel so much at home with that person. This has happened for me with former work colleagues, when there has been an immediate richness in our conversation many years on.

- The best conversations are dynamic and take us in new directions to new conclusions in unexpected ways.

If you can resonate with some of the examples above, then I hope this book is going to be a stimulus to help you enjoy conversation all the more and use it to the best possible effect.

Framework of succeeding chapters

The next chapters illustrate seven types of conversations: listening, encouraging, challenging, short, painful, unresponsive and joyful.

At the start of each chapter are two conversations from the life of Jesus. These provide the touchstone for the rest of the chapter. I view Jesus as a hugely influential role model who dared to be different and dared to use conversation in a variety of very powerful ways. The impact Jesus had in conversation is relevant for people of faith or no faith. His exchanges with other people speak for themselves as examples of the courageous use of conversation.

Each chapter illustrates some general themes based on the two examples from the life of Jesus. It then includes practical illustrations and stories from contemporary life which further illustrate those themes. The chapters conclude with some questions for reflection either by individuals or by groups. At the end of the book are some notes for small groups who might be discussing the content of the chapters.

Chapter 9 is about practical next steps. It uses as its framework the three strands of *engagement*, *discernment* and *stretching* that are evident in the approach Jesus took to conversations. Within these broad categories we look specifically at more detailed practical aspects. The chapter also includes a section on pitfalls to avoid.

In her book *Difficult Conversations*, Anne Dixon talks of the importance of allowing ourselves to be vulnerable in conversation:

> Friendship and intimacy are forged through stumbling, acknowledging responsibility, arguing, caring and engaging together. It takes effort and time ... and honesty. We can only achieve genuine, meaningful communication if we are prepared to take the risk of being open and vulnerable with each other.

Within the family, within your community and within your workplace, the gains of being open and vulnerable in conversation far outweigh the risks. The impact we can have for good through engaging, discerning and stretching is profound. In the range of conversations we have every day – short or unresponsive, painful or joyful – we can raise people's spirits sometimes through our words, sometimes through our presence and sometimes through our eyes and our smiles.

So be brave. Try something new today in the way you share in conversation with others. Share a bit more of yourself. Take some risks and listen to the thoughts and emotions behind the words.

Listening conversations

Francis de Sales, a French Roman Catholic bishop in the early seventeenth century, wrote, 'Half-an-hour's listening is essential except when you are very busy. Then a full hour is needed.' Paul Tillich, the eminent Swiss theologian, said, 'The first duty of love is to listen.' Perhaps the most famous quote about listening is the saying often used with talkative children: 'You have been given two ears and only one tongue so that you might listen twice as much as you speak.' Listening is the essential starting point for understanding.

Jesus' life was busy with teaching but also with listening. The two illustrations below come from opposite ends of his life, the first when he was 12 and the second after his resurrection.

Every year his parents went to Jerusalem for the Feast of the Passover. When he was twelve years old, they went up to the Feast, according to the custom. After the Feast was over, while his parents were returning home, the boy Jesus stayed behind in Jerusalem, but they were unaware of it. Thinking he was in their company, they travelled on for a day. Then they began looking for him among their relatives and friends. When they did not find him, they went back to Jerusalem to look for him.

After three days they found him in the temple courts, sitting among the teachers, listening to them and asking them questions. Everyone who heard him was amazed at his understanding and his answers. When his parents saw him, they were astonished. His mother said to him, 'Son, why have you treated us like this? Your father and I have been anxiously searching for you.'

'Why were you searching for me?' he asked. 'Didn't you know I had to be in my Father's house?' But they did not understand what he was saying to them.

Then he went down to Nazareth with them and was obedient to them. But his mother treasured all these things in her heart. And Jesus grew in wisdom and stature, and in favour with God and men. (Lk. 2.41–52)

The 12-year-old Jesus was fully engaged with the teachers in the temple courts. He was listening to understand. They were fully engrossed, and as a consequence the time passed very quickly. Those around were enlivened by the conversation, amazed at Jesus' understanding and his answers. In listening to the teachers and questioning them, Jesus was growing in wisdom and stature. The starting point was listening, but there was full dialogue because of his understanding and answers.

There was another listening process going on too. Mary must have been exasperated with her wayward 12-year-old. She was very anxious about her lost son and his initial retort did not seem very sympathetic: 'Why were you searching for me?' But amidst the inevitably rather difficult conversation, Mary was listening to Jesus. Luke records that she 'treasured all these things in her heart'. Mary had been doing a lot of listening over the years. After being told of the forthcoming birth of Jesus she sang, 'My soul glorifies the Lord and my spirit rejoices in God my Saviour (Lk. 1. 46)'. After the birth of Jesus in the stable and the arrival of the enthusiastic shepherds, she was amazed at what the shepherds said to her and 'treasured up all these things and pondered them in her heart' (Lk. 2.19). A few days after the birth Simeon said to her, 'A sword will pierce your own soul too' (Lk. 2.35). Mary listened without full understanding, but pondered and treasured all she heard. For her, listening was only to partially understand, but it was no less important to treasure those thoughts.

The second example of a listening conversation is from the time when Jesus met two of the disciples walking on the road to Emmaus.

Now that same day two of them were going to a village called Emmaus, about seven miles from Jerusalem. They were talking with each other about everything that had happened. As they talked and discussed these things with each other, Jesus himself came up and walked along with them; but they were kept from recognising him.

He asked them, 'What are you discussing together as you walk along?'

They stood still, their faces downcast. One of them, named Cleopas, asked him, 'Are you only a visitor to Jerusalem and do not know the things that have happened there in these days?'

'What things?' he asked.

'About Jesus of Nazareth,' they replied. 'He was a prophet, powerful in word and deed before God and all the people. The chief priests and our rulers handed him over to be sentenced to death, and they crucified him; but we had hoped that he was the one who was going to redeem Israel. And what is more, it is the third day since all this took place. In addition, some of our women amazed us. They went to the tomb early this morning but didn't find his body. They came and told us that they had seen a vision of angels, who said he was alive. Then some of our companions went to the tomb and found it just as the women had said, but him they did not see.'

He said to them, 'How foolish you are, and how slow of heart to believe all that the prophets have spoken! Did not the Christ have to suffer these things and then enter his glory?' And beginning with Moses and all the Prophets, he explained to them what was said in all the Scriptures concerning himself.

As they approached the village to which they were going, Jesus acted as if he were going further. But they urged him strongly, 'Stay with us, for it is nearly evening; the day is almost over.' So he went in to stay with them.

When he was at the table with them, he took bread, gave thanks, broke it and began to give it to them. Then their eyes were opened and they recognised him, and he disappeared from their sight. They asked each other, 'Were not our hearts burning within us while he talked with us on the road and opened the Scriptures to us?'

They got up and returned at once to Jerusalem. There they found the Eleven and those with them, assembled together and saying, 'It is true! The Lord has risen and has appeared to Simon.' Then the two told what had happened on the way, and how Jesus was recognised by them when he broke the bread. (Lk. 24. 13–35)

These disciples were talking to each other about everything that had happened over the previous days concerning the crucifixion and resurrection of Jesus. They needed to talk these things through. Jesus walked with them, but they did not recognize him. Jesus asked them open questions about what they were discussing and then began a dialogue with them. He understood the source of their worries and concerns and shared reflections with them from his knowledge of the Old Testament Scriptures.

The two disciples had done all the right things. They were wound up by what had happened. They needed to walk and talk. Jesus was listening to discern their level of understanding. He did not reveal who he was for a long time. They were fully engrossed and did not recognize the stranger who had joined them. After listening to the disciples, Jesus challenged them hard: 'How foolish you are, and how slow of heart to believe all that the prophets have spoken!' The disciples invited him in for supper. When they recognized him they realized that their hearts had been 'burning' within them as they talked together on the road. When Jesus had gone, their immediate response was to return at once to Jerusalem to share their experience with the other disciples.

From these two conversations we can identify some key principles about listening which are relevant to both participants in a listening conversation.

- **Value people**. Jesus valued the knowledge of the people he was talking to in the temple and the companionship of the disciples on the road to Emmaus.
- **Ask questions**. Jesus never stopped asking questions in order to further his understanding and to draw people out.

21

- **Listen to learn and discern**. Jesus was not asking questions for the sake of it. His aim was to discern as clearly as possible the understanding of those with whom he was talking.
- **Be engrossed**. Jesus was fully engrossed with the two disciples as they walked on the road to Emmaus. It was their story he was sharing as he drew out their understanding of recent events.
- **Be fully engaged**. Jesus was giving the teachers in the temple his full, undivided attention, so much so that the time passed very quickly.
- **Bring objectivity**. The boy Jesus asked the teachers key questions. He was discussing in depth to reach a clearer understanding. To the travellers on the road to Emmaus he responded by saying they had been slow of heart in believing what the prophets had spoken.
- **Be enlivened**. In both instance the participants were energized by the conversation.
- **Be surprised**. The disciples on the road to Emmaus were completely taken aback when they realized who had been walking with them. They were astonished by the way Jesus explained the Scriptures to them. Mary was surprised by the reaction of the 12-year-old Jesus, but treasured that surprise in her heart.
- **Walk alongside**. Perhaps the most powerful picture is that of Jesus walking alongside the disciples, showing his empathy with them as they worked through their understanding of what they had experienced.
- **Accept that you won't always understand**. The disciples were wrestling with their own lack of understanding. They had to keep talking through their experiences in Jerusalem. It was hard for them to accept that they did not fully understand what had happened.

Examples of listening

You may well have strong memories of good listening conversations. It is worth reflecting on why they worked so well. I would like to share with you two examples of effective listening.

Many people today work at call centres, where effective listening is a core part of their job. I had a delightful conversation recently with a customer service adviser at a bank. I phoned up the bank and got a series of automated phone messages. Eventually I got through to a 'real person'. Joy at last. I found myself speaking to a delightful lady who was both helpful and reassuring.

When she had given me the answer to my enquiry, I asked her about the type of short conversations she had. She explained that they had detailed procedures to follow; they were trained to build a rapport with people on the end of the telephone. 'You just have to be cheerful,' she said. 'I like being chirpy, so it isn't a problem for me, but I know others find it a real trial to have to be cheerful all the time.' She told me of the four weeks' training she had had and their practice with different types of dialogue. 'You mustn't come over as too wooden: you must demonstrate that you're listening,' she said.

I asked what happened when they had a difficult customer. She said, 'It's important to continue to be professional. The training helps. We've gone through practice dialogues with people who are difficult. You always try to resolve the problem and try to keep chirpy and happy. You accept that sometimes people get out of the wrong side of the bed. Sometimes they have a very good case.'

She said that it was not always easy to listen constructively. 'When somebody's stroppy you can't help but take it a bit personally. You tell yourself that you're doing your best to solve the customer's problem, but if they get cross or angry you feel the pain even though you had no part in creating the specific problem.' She told me that talking to her colleagues was important. They shared their dilemmas in dealing with customers.

She said that if a customer wanted to talk and extend the conversation, perhaps because they were lonely, she responded in a friendly way but had to bring the conversation to a close. She had targets to meet and her salary was being paid for by the company, and therefore long conversations were out of the question. But she always wanted to leave a customer feeling good and cheerful and to demonstrate that she had listened. At this point I sensed that I should move on! Her final words were, 'I like being chirpy and if I can listen effectively and help somebody resolve the problem, that makes me feel good.'

My second example is a story shared with me by a work colleague. It was a few years ago, but the effect has stayed with him very strongly ever since. This is John's story:

Coming home late – 21.20 from Waterloo in London a few weeks before Christmas – I was reading an evening newspaper and feeling a bit low. I had some difficult issues at work, I'd been working long hours and I was dog tired. If truth were told, I was feeling sorry for myself. For the past few weeks, life had seemed hard.

The guard began to blow his whistle and a young man, about 22 or 23, snatched open the door alongside me. He was unkempt, to put it kindly, with long dirty hair and a badly stained yellow anorak. In one hand he clutched a rather ratty rucksack, while the other held a can of extra-strength lager. He swore lustily as his rucksack caught in the doorway, attracting disapproving attention from the entire carriage of this old slam-door train. The clanking sounds from the rucksack as he threw it onto the seat told me that he was not likely to run out of liquid sustenance during this particular journey. He hurled himself down into the seat opposite me, slamming the door with a huge crash, and looked around him.

'B★★★★★ds!' he said loudly to no one in particular and took a swig from his can. This was evidently not the first he'd sampled, for the smell of drink was overpowering. The man on the other end of the three-person seat opposite me immediately got up, grabbed his case and moved off down the carriage. My new travelling companion sneered, 'That's right! F★★★ off out of here, you f★★★★★★ w★★★★★!'

All around, heads sank lower behind the evening papers. It began to look as if this was not going to be as relaxing a journey home as I'd hoped. The train began to move out and the young man shuffled across in the seat and swung his legs up onto the seat on my side, the heels of his Doc Marten boots alongside me. I sighed and he immediately bristled. 'What's up with you then, mate?'

'I'd like you not to put your feet on my seat, please – it'll make it dirty and that'll rub off on my new coat.' I kept my voice neutral, but met his eye and tried to look disarming. I had no wish to start a fight.

We stared at each other for a few seconds. Then, thankfully, he put his boots back onto the floor. 'Expensive, is it?'

'What?'

'Your coat. Cost a packet, did it?'

I shook my head. It hadn't. 'I bought it in a sale. In Guildford – that's where I live.'

He asked a couple more questions – what did I do,

did I have any kids, that sort of thing. I gave short, factual, careful answers.

With the conversation he seemed to be losing the aggression of a few minutes earlier, so I thought I'd keep going. 'Where do you live? Are you off home?' I asked him. I wondered how he would react, but to my surprise he lowered his lager can and stared at the floor. Then he began to talk. It wasn't exactly a flowing conversation, so the account which follows came out in fits and starts, prompted by occasional questions and sympathetic nods from me. It became clear that he *really* wanted to talk. The gist of his story, arranged into some sort of chronology, was this.

His name was Glen – though that was the last thing about him I discovered – and he wasn't sure where home was any more. He had lived in Portsmouth, but when he was 17 his parents had divorced, his father had moved out and his mother had taken up with a new man. He'd left home shortly afterwards to move in with his dad, but they had fallen out since Glen couldn't get a job and pay his way. His father had thrown him out. An aunt had offered to give him lodging until he could get on his feet, but he had taken himself off to London. Since then he had been living there, sometimes with temporary friends and once, for a while, sleeping rough. He had found only temporary jobs and at the minute had no money, no job, no girlfriend, no home and, from what he told me, not much in the way of prospects. At times as he talked his eyes filled with tears. But, he assured me, he was 'OK'; he could 'take care' of himself.

So what was he going to do now, I wondered? He was heading back to Portsmouth and was going to his aunt, not so much because he wanted to, but because he had run out of options. Once Christmas was over he was going to do something different, though he didn't have much idea of what that something might be. He was not the most articulate of men. He swore a lot, talking without much self-pity but with a wry gallows humour.

We reached Guildford. 'I have to get off here,' I said. 'By the way, what's your name?'

'Glen,' he replied. He held out his hand and I took it. 'Thanks for listening, mate.' The edgy aggression seemed to have been diverted.

I gathered up my paper and briefcase, said goodbye and stepped off the train. As I walked towards the exit one of my fellow travellers, overtaking, said, 'If you don't mind me saying so, I thought you handled that youth very well.' I didn't bother to reply, but shook my head. Both of us had been guilty of 'judging the book by its cover' rather than its content. For my part I felt quite chastened, because whatever I might have been thinking at Waterloo, I had precious little to complain about.

Part of the lesson of this story is that it is vital to keep listening and not make premature judgements. The importance of holding back is reinforced by something told to me by a friend about one of his colleagues, who had a very bad stutter. When listening to his colleague there was always a temptation to jump in and complete his sentences. What my friend had learnt was that it was really important to give his colleague space and let him say what he wanted to say. He often came out with quite surprising views. For my friend this was an object lesson in listening properly and not jumping to conclusions about what people think.

Writers on listening

Much has been written about the art of listening. Dietrich Bonhoeffer, a German pastor executed by the Nazi regime, wrote thoughtfully about listening when in his prison cell. He wrote in *Life Together*,

> The first service that one owes to others in the fellowship consists in listening to them. Many people are looking for an ally that will listen. They do not find it among Christians, because these Christians are talking where they should be listening. But he who can no longer listen to his brothers will soon be no longer listening to God either; he will be doing nothing but prattle in the presence of God too. Anyone who cannot listen long and patiently will presently be talking beside the point and be never really speaking to others. There is a kind of listening with half an ear that presumes already to know what the other person has to say. It is an impatient, inattentive listening, that despises the brother and is only waiting for a chance to speak and thus get rid of the other person.

Bonhoeffer's focus is that listening can be a greater service than speaking: 'We should listen with the ears of God that we may speak the Word of God.'

Ann Long's influential book *Listening* was published in 1990. In his foreword to the book Gerard Hughes says, 'Listening is an art which we can only acquire by practice.' Ann Long says that good listeners develop and grow by learning to reflect on the questions and difficulties that inevitably arise in the listening relationship. She uses three images to describe the ministry of listening as gift, hospitality and healing. For her, 'being listened to can feel a great gift, being listened to and heard an even greater one. When listened to and heard in this way, we know that we matter!' She describes listening as being about hospitality, the offering to someone of space in which to feel welcomed, met and safe, free to be themselves, free to be listened to and heard. Then she sets out six dimensions which make up a good listener's offering and skill:

- **Respect:** giving value to the other person, affirming them as unique.
- **Genuineness:** being real and open rather than playing a role, and not play-acting at listening.
- **Empathy:** which is not 'to feel like' but 'to feel with'. It is about seeing the world through the other person's eyes, being accurately aware of their feelings and attempting to put them into words.
- **Concreteness:** helping a person to avoid vagueness and to be specific.
- **Confrontation:** this is not about trying to catch someone out, but is about firmly and carefully enabling a person to become aware of the discrepancies in their thinking.
- **Immediacy:** which is about being fully aware of how you are being experienced as a listener.

Henri Nouwen called listening 'the highest form of hospitality', of a sort that does not set out to 'change' people but offers them space where change can happen. The offering of personal space through listening enables healing to take place.

Jonathan Sacks wrote an article about listening in *The Times* on 14 December 2002. He wrote:

What an underrated art listening is. Sometimes it is the greatest gift we can give to a troubled soul. It is an act of focused attention. It means being genuinely open to another person, prepared to enter their world, their perspective, their pain. It does not mean we have a solution to their problem. There are some problems that cannot be solved. They can only be lived through, so that time itself heals the rupture or loss. When we listen we share the burden so its weight can be borne. There are times when friendship calls simply for a human presence, a listening ear and an understanding heart so that soul can unburden to soul.

Michael Mitton has written a thoughtful book on *A Heart to Listen*. He too focuses on the importance of healing flowing from listening.

Most of us get by in everyday life through fairly superficial conversations serving the purpose of keeping us in touch with others and getting things done. Even at this level, good listening can make a world of difference. It is at the deep, and personal level, however, that the cost of poor listening can be so high and the effects of good listening can be so healing.

Every person has stories within them that need telling. At certain points in life, they can feel an urgent need to tell one of these stories. Somebody who is grieving, for example, often wants to tell their story of loss. They probably won't know why they need to tell the story: it is simply there, at the back of their throat, and it must be spoken out. 'Talking it out' is nearly always a very important part of the therapy needed by somebody wounded by loss. It is a sobering thought that there are parts of society where people have no idea what it is like to be listened to. Because they are not listened to, they often have to resort to screaming and violence.

Mitton tells the story of a residential listening course for clergy, which he led. One vicar spoke movingly, saying that when he first started out in the ordained ministry he did listen to people. Some time ago, however, he took the decision to listen no longer, because he could not bear to hear people's problems when he could not think of any solutions. During the listening course that vicar had a 'conversion moment' when he suddenly discovered that it was OK to listen without having a solution to the problem being described. Although listening is not specifically about solutions, it is far from passive. For Mitton,

> Attentive listening is creating space – it is constructive. It is not sitting passively in front of a verbal water jet. It is actively applying often intense concentration to facilitate the person we are listening to, to help them move on in their journey.

Kay Lindahl has put together a set of 40 reflections under the title *The Sacred Art of Listening*. She talks about listening beyond words. She refers to the 'qualities of deep listening' and 'listening for essence'. She advises that when listening, we should suspend assumptions. We can learn to recognize assumptions by noticing when we get upset or annoyed by something someone else is saying. We should listen without judgement, aiming to come to an understanding of the other without determining whether they are good, bad, right or wrong.

Constructive listening is about recognizing the importance of other people's views, identifying a purpose in most discussions, being sensitive about when to shut up and bringing conversations to a conclusion in a way that is positive and not abrupt. Constructive listening is not eavesdropping, nor is it just allowing someone to meander endlessly about, being defensive, hiding or disguising your own personality or feelings, or deferring to all and sundry.

Essential to good listening is the use of questions that elicit a thoughtful, open response. When a good question is asked, a genuine and worthwhile exchange takes place between two people. When you ask a good question, both you and the other person know you are listening. Juliet Erickson, in *The Art of Persuasion*, says that 'asking questions is like dancing. Do it wrong and you'll tread on your partner's toes, cramp their style or embarrass them. Get it right and you move together so easily that the whole thing is a pleasure. Even though you are still leading it is so subtle that your partner is barely aware of it and is happy to follow.' She suggests that good questions show you are prepared, are asked with genuine interest, get the real answer to what you have asked, help your listener gain insight into their situation, allow you to move towards the best possible solution, are appropriate and never intrusive and build rapport and understanding.

Questions are often described as closed or open. Closed questions are brief, pointed and invite specific information. There is a place for closed questions when time is short and you need to get down to specifics. They usually involve phrases such as: When? Where? How many? How much? How long? Who? What? Closed questions can be very useful for bringing things to a conclusion when it is right to move the conversation on. The question 'So what are you going to do next?' can help focus action at the end of a listening conversation.

Open questions, by contrast, invite long answers and are

ideal when exploring thoughts, feelings and attitudes. When open questions are asked in a friendly and interested way, they often result in revealing answers. Open questions use phrases such as: What do you think about ...? What are your feelings about ...? Why? How? What matters? Could you elaborate on ...? Tell me about...

The orthodoxy tends to be that open questions are the best ones to ask in a listening conversation. My perspective is that the ideal is a combination of open and closed questions. Open questions are crucial to open up discussions, to glean information and to demonstrate that you are listening. But closed questions can be very powerful when it comes to moving the action on into next steps.

Effective listening is not about complete silence. Juliet Erickson includes the following as good practice:

- **Validate**. Validating what someone has said makes them feel good, while affirming that you have heard and understood what they are saying. We often withhold compliments through embarrassment, stinginess or thoughtfulness, but 'What a good suggestion' can be a very affirming comment in a listening conversation.
- **Pause**. Allow someone time to think, to give a more considered answer. Pausing after the answer can also encourage some further development.
- **Ask one question at a time**. Take a deep breath, slow down and ask one at a time if a deluge of questions floods into your mind.
- **Summarize**. Summaries are relevant not only at the end of a conversation but at key points within a conversation. They can help mark the 'completion' of parts of a conversation and allow for a smoother transition. They can also provide reassurance that as a listener you have heard and understood what has been said.

I frequently work with a colleague who uses the following exercise to demonstrate the importance of good listening skills. The exercise has three rounds.

- In Round 1 both people speak simultaneously for 30 seconds about their journey to work.
- In Round 2 one person acts as a listener and takes up the position of a rock (no eye contact, no movement, no sound). The other person speaks for about a minute about 'the things I enjoy in my job'. After a minute, the two participants switch roles and repeat.
- In Round 3 one person acts as a listener, but this time is free to use normal eye contact and body language, but no whole words, only encouraging sounds (i.e. 'um', 'ah', 'hm'). The other person speaks for about a minute on 'the things I find difficult about my job'. After a minute they change roles and repeat.

After each round the participants discuss what happened. How easy was it to listen? How easy was it to speak? What were the learning points? This is always a very lively and enjoyable exercise. In Round 1 people find it very difficult to speak and listen at the same time. In Round 2 the absence of any facial response from the listener has a devastating effect on the ability of the person who is talking to be animated in what they say. In Round 3 the use of normal eye contact and body language is such an encouragement that the conversation flows much more effectively. Simple exercises like this demonstrate how important it is not to interrupt or talk over other people. The engagement of the whole person in a conversation is vital, and not just the words we say.

Next steps

So how can we listen effectively? At the start of this chapter we identified some key principles for listening based on conversations Jesus had, and below are some concluding reflections on these principles, taking into account what we have also learnt from our own conversations and from written wisdom on the art of listening.

- **Value people**. Our preference will be to want to spend time with people we value. The more we value people, the more we will want to spend time with them and listen to them. How much do we value our colleagues, neighbours and acquaintances?
- **Ask questions**. Experiment with different sorts of questions. Ask lots of open questions. Observe the questions other people ask and see which ones work and elicit fuller answers. Keep a note of what type of questions work and use them on future occasions.
- **Listen to learn and discern**. The start of listening is wanting to discern why someone thinks, believes, feels as they do. If we go into each conversation wanting to learn through our listening, we will be open to be influenced and changed. Allowing listening conversation to be dynamic, so we are receptive to change, makes us vulnerable but provides so much potential enrichment.
- **Be engrossed**. Politicians can be brilliant at this. I have worked with government ministers of different political parties who were superb at being fully engrossed in discussion. Whether it was Michael Portillo or John Redwood (ministers in John Major's government) talking to adults in rundown housing estates, or Ivan Lewis or David Miliband (ministers in Tony Blair's government) talking to young people, they rapidly

won the confidence of those with whom they were talking. Too often we can dismiss politicians and not fully appreciate the skills they have developed working with constituents. Unless they do become genuinely engrossed in conversation they will be rapidly written off as charlatans. We can learn from their skills, both when their approach works well and when it is less successful.

- **Be fully engaged**. Observe people who are very good at this. When Barbara Bush visited schools in London as the wife of the then President of the USA I spent a couple of hours in her company. She was brilliant at being fully engaged with all the young people she met. The good listener will play back the name of the individual they are talking to and demonstrate through their eyes and their body language that they are fully immersed in the conversation. Consciously smile as you listen and nod to demonstrate that you have heard. Make sure that you really are giving your full and undivided attention.

- **Bring objectivity**. Whatever the heightened emotions of a particular situation, objectivity is a great gift. Whilst absorbing the emotions, keep the rational part of your brain working. What is the real level of pain? Is this as big a crisis as it appears? What are the logical next steps? It may well not be advisable to present the rational, objective answer immediately. There will be a right moment to put issues into a wider perspective. Keeping that detachment and objectivity is crucial to effective listening: you need to be absorbed in the issue but not completely absorbed. If someone is stuck in the mud, the person with the helping hand needs to try to stay on firm ground while reaching out to provide support.

- **Be enlivened**. The best way of fully embracing the issues someone faces is to stand in their shoes. Imagine yourself in their situation facing the dilemmas and pressures they face. How would you react? What would be your anxieties and sources of strength? In this way you can share more of someone's pain or joy. As you talk with someone, be willing to share fully in their joy or hurt. Allow that to enliven you. Watch your own emotions and reactions. They can be such an important barometer. If you begin to feel depressed, so is the person you are talking with.

- **Be surprised**. Do not just assume that the conversation will take a predictable course. Be curious. Assume that each conversation is dynamic. Be ready to be surprised as you understand more and more about the situation and the person you are listening to. Be surprised by the pleasure, pain or joy you are sharing in that conversation.

- **Walk alongside**. When I worked for the government in the north-east of England there were riots on two housing estates. The then Secretary of State for the Environment, Michael Heseltine, paid a visit which we did not announce to the press. I walked with him through the streets, meeting individual residents who showed him round some of the destruction. It was as they walked together that he showed empathy for these people. They felt supported and encouraged by him as he listened to their stories. Walking alongside involved some questions, some quietness and some careful reflection about next steps. Walking alongside is such a crucial part of listening, because it creates a sense of travelling together in the same direction. How might you walk alongside people more effectively?

- **Accept that you won't always understand**. Being effective in conversation does not need understanding everything that is said. There needs to be enough understanding for some quiet response, but sometimes the speakers themselves will not fully understand and need to keep articulating to try to crystallize some of their own conclusions. Sometimes listeners will have insights that help the speakers understand what they are saying. On some occasions listening will involve very partial understanding and no solutions, but that does not mean it is a waste of time.

Questions for reflection

The questions below are intended as a prompt for reflection either individually or in small groups. They are a starting point. Be adventurous in the way you reflect on them.

1. In what ways is the approach Jesus took in listening to the teachers in the temple and to the disciples on the road to Emmaus helpful to you?
2. Can you share any stories of conversations where you have listened and where the individual has found that helpful?
3. What do you find most difficult about listening?
4. How might you experiment with different types of questions?
5. How can you best take forward the key principles of listening?
    - Value people.
    - Ask questions.

- Listen to learn and discern.
- Be engrossed.
- Be fully engaged.
- Bring objectivity.
- Be enlivened.
- Be surprised.
- Walk alongside.
- Accept you won't always understand.

Encouraging conversations 3

Have you ever been lifted by being encouraged in conversation? Just a gentle word of praise, thanks or encouragement can make such a difference. Perhaps it has come from an unexpected source. It has not mattered that it is a repeated message. Repetition of genuine words of encouragement has such a powerful effect on us. The most effective encouragement reinforces the good in us and enables us to face up to difficult issues. We can never be generous enough in our encouragement to others.

The nineteenth-century poet Gerard Manley Hopkins wrote, 'There is a point with me in matters of any size when I must absolutely have encouragement as much as crops rain.' Encouragement has been called the oxygen of the soul. Encouragement is crucial for our very existence. It is just as important as rain or oxygen. Without encouragement we wither and die. Paul was very explicit in writing to the Romans, 'We have different gifts, according to the grace given us. If a man's gift is ... encouraging, let him encourage' (Rom. 12.6).

There are many examples of Jesus engaged in encouraging conversations, although they often have a challenging edge. The two selected here are his conversation with the Samaritan woman at the well and a conversation with his disciples part-way through his ministry.

The Pharisees heard that Jesus was gaining and baptising more disciples than John, although in fact it was not Jesus who baptised, but his disciples. When the Lord learned of this, he left Judea and went back once more to Galilee.

Now he had to go through Samaria. So he came to a town in Samaria called Sychar, near the plot of ground Jacob had given to his son Joseph. Jacob's well was there, and Jesus, tired as he was from the journey, sat down by the well. It was about the sixth hour.

When a Samaritan woman came to draw water, Jesus said to her, 'Will you give me a drink?' (His disciples had gone into the town to buy food.)

The Samaritan woman said to him, 'You are a Jew and I am a Samaritan woman. How can you ask me for a drink?' (For Jews do not associate with Samaritans.)

Jesus answered her, 'If you knew the gift of God and who it is that asks you for a drink, you would have asked him and he would have given you living water.'

'Sir,' the woman said, 'you have nothing to draw with and the well is deep. Where can you get this living water? Are you greater than our father Jacob, who gave us the well and drank from it himself, as did also his sons and his flocks and herds?'

Jesus answered, 'Everyone who drinks this water will be thirsty again, but whoever drinks the water I give him will never thirst. Indeed, the water I give him will become in him a spring of water welling up to eternal life.'

The woman said to him, 'Sir, give me this water so that I won't get thirsty and have to keep coming here to draw water.'

He told her, 'Go, call your husband and come back.'

'I have no husband,' she replied.

Jesus said to her, 'You are right when you say you have no husband. The fact is, you have had five husbands, and the man you now have is not your husband. What you have just said is quite true.'

'Sir,' the woman said, 'I can see that you are a prophet. Our fathers worshipped on this mountain, but you Jews claim that the place where we must worship is in Jerusalem.'

Jesus declared, 'Believe me, woman, a time is coming when you will worship the Father neither on this mountain nor in Jerusalem. You Samaritans worship what you do not know; we worship what we do know, for salvation is from the Jews. Yet a time is coming and has now come when the true worshippers will worship the Father in spirit and truth, for they are the kind of worshippers the Father seeks. God is spirit, and his worshippers must worship in spirit and in truth.'

The woman said, 'I know that Messiah' (called Christ) 'is coming. When he comes, he will explain everything to us.'

Then Jesus declared, 'I who speak to you am he.' (Jn 4.1–26)

Jesus was on a journey and arrived at a Samaritan town called Sychar. He sat by the well. When the Samaritan woman came to draw water the conversation began with a question from Jesus, 'Will you give me a drink?' The Jewish and Samaritan people were often not on speaking terms. Asking for a drink from a Samaritan was unusual, and asking to receive something from a Samaritan woman was even more unusual. Jesus initiated the conversation in an unexpected way, and this elicited a surprised reaction from the Samaritan woman. Jesus then stretches the thinking of the woman by talking about living water. She challenges him, and Jesus responds by saying that whoever drinks the living water will never thirst. He asks perceptive questions about her marital status and shows understanding for her situation. He talks of the differences between Samaritans and Jews being a thing of the past when true worshippers will worship the Father in spirit and truth.

The encouragement Jesus offered came from him asking to receive water from the Samaritan woman, stretching her thinking about living water, being perceptive in understanding her family situation and stressing that Samaritans and Jews worshipped the same God. It was not an easy conversation. Jesus asked direct questions about her family and challenged her understanding about worship.

In the second passage Jesus is encouraging his disciples.

'Do not let your hearts be troubled. Trust in God; trust also in me. In my Father's house are many rooms; if it were not so, I would have told you. I am going there to prepare a place for you. And if I go and prepare a place for you, I will come back and take you to be with me that you also may be where I am. You know the way to the place where I am going.'

Thomas said to him, 'Lord, we don't know where you are going, so how can we know the way?'

Jesus answered, 'I am the way and the truth and the life. No one comes to the Father except through me. If you really knew me, you would know my Father as well. From now on, you do know him and have seen him.'

Philip said, 'Lord, show us the Father and that will be enough for us.'

Jesus answered: 'Don't you know me, Philip, even after I have been among you such a long time? Anyone who has seen me has seen the Father. How can you say,

"Show us the Father"? Don't you believe that I am in the Father, and that the Father is in me? The words I say to you are not just my own. Rather, it is the Father, living in me, who is doing his work. Believe me when I say that I am in the Father and the Father is in me; or at least believe on the evidence of the miracles themselves. I tell you the truth, anyone who has faith in me will do what I have been doing. He will do even greater things than these, because I am going to the Father. And I will do whatever you ask in my name, so that the Son may bring glory to the Father. You may ask me for anything in my name, and I will do it.' (Jn 14.1–14)

The context of this passage is important. In the previous chapter Jesus has had intense discussions with the disciples. He has dramatically washed his disciples' feet and predicted his own betrayal and then Peter's denial. It must have been an emotional roller-coaster in this period leading up to the crucifixion. Against this background, what the disciples needed was positive encouragement. The chapter begins with the positive injunction, 'Do not let your hearts be troubled. Trust in God; trust also in me.' He talks of the many rooms in his Father's house and promises that he is going there 'to prepare a place for you'.

Thomas says rather plaintively, 'We don't know where you are going, so how can we know the way?' Then come the encouraging words from Jesus, 'I am the way and the truth and the life,' as he points the way to God the Father. These words, like so many from Jesus, are both supportive and challenging. Jesus asserts, 'If you really knew me, you would know my Father as well.' The words may be encouraging, but there is also an expectation that the disciples should try to know Jesus even more, so that their understanding of God the Father increases too.

A similar discussion takes place with Philip, who asks whether it is possible to see the Father. Jesus gently responds, 'Don't you know me, Philip, even after I have been among you such a long time? Anyone who has seen me has seen the Father.' He encourages them to believe him when he says that he is in the Father and the Father is in him.

Jesus' responses to Thomas and Philip are patient and clear. He does not ignore the disciples' questions – he gives a positive response to them, affirming his relationship with God the Father. Yet again there is a challenging edge. Jesus is very clear in saying, 'Anyone who has faith in me will do what I have been doing.' He stretches this even further by saying, 'he will do even greater things than these'. The words of encouragement were important, but they were just the first part in the process of challenging the disciples to raise their expectations.

From these encouraging conversations we can outline some central themes.

- **Intimacy**. Jesus spoke one to one with the Samaritan woman, with Thomas and with Philip. He gave each of them time to speak with him directly.
- **Trust**. Jesus says to the Samaritan woman, 'Believe me.' To the disciples he says, 'Trust also in me.' Trust is at the absolute centre of these relationships.
- **Openness**. Jesus initiated the conversation with the Samaritan woman and the initial conversation with the disciples.
- **Surprise**. Jesus took the Samaritan woman by surprise by speaking at length to her. He took the disciples by surprise by coming out with profound and memorable phrases. The element of surprise reinforced the encouragement.

- **Understanding the context**. Jesus clearly understands the context of a Samaritan woman who feels uneasy giving something to a Jew. He understands very clearly that the disciples are feeling troubled. His words of encouragement speak directly into the context of his hearers. He demonstrates empathy in the way he relates to his hearers.
- **Reassurance**. The words of Jesus are not about lecturing his hearers but about reassuring them that he wants to have a thoughtful, reflective conversation with them.
- **Stretching**. He stretches their thinking. He talks with the Samaritan woman about living water and with the disciples about his relationship with God the Father. He uses their questions not to give bland reassurance but to help them understand another dimension of God's purpose.
- **Sense of direction**. Jesus makes it clear to the Samaritan woman that true worshippers will worship the Father in spirit and truth with cultural backgrounds an irrelevance. To the disciples he gives a clear sense of direction by saying that he is the way, the truth and the life. Jesus provides clarity about what is important.
- **Challenge**. There is always a hard edge. Encouragement is accompanied by expectation: his hearers are to move on and grow in their understanding and commitment. He is always stretching his hearers to raise their expectations.

Do we encourage enough?

Do we encourage people enough? Can we ever encourage people enough? A friend challenged me recently, saying that she had not received many encouraging words from me in recent weeks. I have tried to make amends since. She is a very self-contained and influential lady. I had not thought that she needed encouragement. What that little exchange showed me was that we are all in need of regular encouragement. However independent minded people might look, encouragement is essential for their well-being.

For a period of five years Estelle Morris worked as a minister in the Education Department, initially as a junior minister and then as Secretary of State. She was always positive and encouraging. I never heard her say an evil word about anyone. She came under severe political pressure because of problems with the grading of some examination papers by one examination board. The decisions were entirely a matter for the examination board and not for her. This did not stop the media attacking her day after day. In the midst of this welter of criticism she took time out to encourage the two officials who had been particularly close to the initial action. She spent time with each of them, one to one, full of words of encouragement. When she resigned there were many tears among her officials who had come to love her dearly, largely because of this strong sense of encouragement which she never gave up, even when she was under extreme pressure. The characteristics of her encouragement were its regularity, its openness and its warmth.

Be ready to be surprised

Sometimes conversations can become encouraging in ways you least expected. On one occasion I had been speaking at a conference in Sunningdale to the west of London. I needed to make a quick getaway to be at another event 15 miles away. My time was short. The receptionist phoned the taxi company, who said that a taxi would be there in five minutes. Fifteen minutes later there was still no taxi. I walked around to keep calm. Twenty minutes passed, then 25 minutes. I told myself I would not speak acerbically to the taxi driver. At last, after 30 minutes, the taxi arrived. I climbed in. My mouth opened to complain about the delay, but when the driver explained that he had only been told about this pick-up five minutes earlier, I instinctively believed him. He was a kindly Muslim gentleman.

We talked about the range of conversations he had as a taxi driver. He said that he tended to keep quiet and let people do the talking. He learnt lots of different things from passengers who wanted to talk. Sometimes they were joyful, sometimes in pain. Sad people often shared their agonies with him. His was a listening ear with perhaps a far greater impact for good than he had realized. He was a natural encourager.

'What do you like to talk to your passengers about?' I asked him.

'Oh, not much,' he said. 'I'm happy to listen.' Then he began to talk about his family. He had four grown-up children, of whom he was very proud. Gradually he opened up about his youngest child. His son was mentally handicapped. He could not walk, had to be fed and could hardly communicate. He needed constant care. The driver talked about his son with huge affection. There was a strong emotional bond which tied them together. In spite of this sadness, it was clear that my driver was a proud father for whom his family was more important than anything else.

Perhaps because words were not at the centre of the conversations he had with his son, he did not waste words in conversation with his passengers. He was genuinely happy to listen. I felt honoured that in our brief conversation he had told me his own story about the pain and pleasure of communicating with his son. He was anxious to emphasize that there are joyful and encouraging moments even when communication is very limited.

There are various people we pass each day and talk to only very briefly. Sometimes spending longer in conversation with one or two of these people can bring new revelations. At the university college where I am a frequent visitor there is a very special person on the reception desk. I try to spend time with him when I can because he is always such a source of encouragement. He is always cheerful. He looks a bit bashed around by life, which is not surprising given his love of riding on his motorbike. He has great gifts of listening and curiosity. The students chat to him as they pick up their keys. Some come for a natter because they are feeling a bit down. Others are a little bored and welcome his jollity. He is full of pictures and stories. He tells me, 'All humour is visual, so I have a feast of stories and pictures to share.' The students appreciate his humour. He admits to being an aimless raconteur, but says it makes them feel better. The students tell me he is wonderful. His conversation is full of quotes from Lewis Carroll, 'Of shoes and ships and sealing wax, of cabbages and kings . . .'

There is a great deal of curiosity in his approach. One of the joys of being on the reception desk is that you are busy one moment and not the next. When all is quiet he dives into the Internet and follows his current interest. He has a wealth of knowledge about physics. He told me once about a student who had come to talk to him about a physics problem and how they had worked it out together. What pleasure that discussion had given him. He is not just the doorman. He is a friend, a source of good practical sense, a source of advice and above all a huge source of encouragement: people feel better for having talked with him. In return he feels greatly valued by the students.

I asked him once where these gifts of conversation came from. 'Well,' he said, 'I ran a pub for 23 years. I enjoyed the richness of the conversations. When two people were sat separately alone in the pub I used to get them talking together.' It was so obvious to him that people in the pub on their own were often feeling lonely and needed conversation. He gained such pleasure when he introduced two people and they began to enjoy their discussion together over a pint. Working at the college reception is a fulfilment of the skills he has developed in conversation and curiosity. He has a crucial role in college life. He is an encourager in conversation, not through the intensity of giving specific positive words, but through his ability to listen, his visual humour, his laugh and his strong sense of curiosity. He is an immensely powerful influence for good.

My doorman friend is not a one-off. In one sense he is unique. His laugh is definitely unique. But there are many people like him around. They get on with life encouraging people who come and share with them. It is our loss when we ignore such people, because they could provide us with a wealth of encouragement.

Part of the joy of living is being ready to meet new people and to be surprised and encouraged by them. If every new conversation is a source of curiosity, we can both encourage and be encouraged by that exploration. Last June I was telephoned out of the blue by a lady from a government department asking if I could spend time the following day working one to one with people on a development programme. Since then she and I have had many conversations. They have always been encouraging and have often been challenging. We have, for example, had firm and challenging conversations about how much the company I work for was going to charge! She has pushed me to do new and different things in working with various groups of people.

The joy of those challenging conversations is that we share many common interests. We both believe passionately in helping individuals to grow through stretching their thinking and putting high-potential people into new and different situations. When we see people grow we get immense satisfaction out of their development. My friend is a devout Roman Catholic for whom a pilgrimage to Lourdes recently was a particularly enriching experience. What is so special about our working relationship is that one minute we are talking about the development programme, the next about practical details for a forthcoming course, the next about costs, and the next about the importance of a shared belief in God's goodness. Openness and challenge go hand in hand and through it all we are a profound source of encouragement to each other. At the heart of this encouragement is the challenge we give each other. Because there is a strong relationship of encouragement, we can be robust in the way we stretch each other's thinking.

As I prepared this book a number of people have shared stories of being surprised by encouraging conversations. A member of our church congregation had been receiving chemotherapy and had then been in hospital suffering from exhaustion. He looked frail but cheerful. We welcomed him back with a round of applause. When he and I spoke after the service he was obviously so pleased to be back in the community he knew and loved so much. He talked of the wonderful care of the nurses, their cheerfulness and good humour. In hospital he was in a room on his own. He waited for the nurses to arrive, and for his visitors to come. He was conscious that we take for granted that opportunity to pass the time of day and have brief conversations with many different people. He decided late one night to read John's Gospel right through. At midnight a nurse came in to do a blood test and noticed him reading his Bible. 'Are you a believer too?' she asked.

'Yes,' said my friend.

The nurse then said, 'Shall we pray together?'

So the ebullient Pentecostal nurse and my rather con-servative Anglican friend (a former church treasurer) prayed together. That was a very special conversation which my friend will long remember. It was the joy of being encouraged by a complete stranger which lifted his spirits.

Sources of encouragement

Encouragement is a two-way process. We can always be a source of encouragement to others, but we also need to allow ourselves to be encouraged by others. Who are your sources of encouragement? I am sure there are people who stand out from your past and your present. Here are some notable encouragers from my past:

- A geography teacher who believed in me and encouraged me to apply to university.
- The principal of Regent College, Vancouver, who encouraged me to be a lay Christian in the secular world and to take on ever more challenging responsibilities within government.
- My first boss in a government department, who helped to shake away the inferiority complex of a northerner in the capital.

These individuals all encouraged me and challenged me to raise my sights and be courageous.

The following people are my current encouragers:

- A long-standing work colleague of over 30 years who always encourages and always expects me to be learning from what has gone well and what has gone less well.
- A young man of 18 who has wonderful skills of empathy and encouragement for someone nearly 40 years older.
- Our three children, who put up with Dad and are always so encouraging.

A rather different source of encouragement comes from two friends who are doctors. For many years they worked in Africa, returning to Canada when their children were of secondary school age. In their late 50s they went back to the Congo as doctors. What wonderful courage they show to be working in the Third World again. It has not all been encouraging for them. They returned to the original hospital at Nyankunde where they had worked a decade earlier. Shortly after they arrived the town and hospital were devastated by rebel forces and they had to move to Oichia, to a hospital with poorer facilities. They have continued nonetheless with a regular round of surgery and nursing training. Their determination and fortitude are wonderfully impressive. They lost all the worldly possessions they had in the Congo when their house was destroyed, but this has not dampened their commitment to Africa or the compassion and generosity they bring to their work. When we meet them they want to encourage us, but their very presence and their stories are powerful sources of encouragement in themselves.

Are there parallel stories of encouragement that stay with you and challenge you? Are there stories that you can share with others, passing on those sources of encouragement to them?

Encouragement is not just something we do with our words and eyes: it is something we do with our whole being. Mirroring is something we all do daily with friends and family without even being aware that we do it. By becoming consciously aware of the power of mirroring we can be even more encouraging in the way we relate to people. Mirroring is a key to the way we use body language. When you are comfortable with someone, you may well adopt a similar position to theirs. If they are sitting and you are standing, you might feel awkward, so you sit down. Mirroring is the way we match the gestures of another person when we feel at ease with them. When we mirror somebody and help them feel at ease, we can more easily convey messages of encouragement to them. It is part of creating intimacy and reassurance. If we want to be encouraging to others, a starting point is to mirror their posture and body language. Experiment with this and you will find that it can have a dramatic effect.

Conversations are not only the verbal communication that takes place between us and someone else. Inner conversations are also vitally important, and they have the power to be a source of encouragement or very destructive. Some people may have conversations with themselves out loud, for instance while competing on the sports field. These may be chastising or encouraging. Some people have a very rich inner life and will mull over problems and thoughts using inner conversation. Their communication with others may be economic as a result.

If our inner conversations are encouraging, we are more likely to be encouraging in conversation with others. Often, however, we are captive to the nature of inner conversations that happen particularly if we lack confidence. To some extent we can train ourselves to have inner conversations that are helpful rather than unhelpful. Our gloomiest inner conversations are likely to take place in the middle of the night. Our most positive inner conversations may well happen after we have been with people we love. When gloom descends inside, reminding ourselves of God's love for us and the love of our friends can begin to bring some light and relief. Encouraging ourselves is an essential part of us being able to encourage others.

Saying goodbye

A crucial part of encouragement is how we say goodbye. Are these final conversations routine, or do they leave each person going away encouraged? It is not always the precise words but the warmth of the goodbye that matters. These farewell conversations at the school gate, at the airport, at university or at a retirement party are an essential part of moving on. As we move into the next phase of a day, a year or a life, that sense of being encouraged onwards is so important. The farewell encouragement is perhaps the most significant short discussion that takes place in our lives. If we let these situations pass by, we are missing a golden opportunity to leave an indelible mark of encouragement.

Sometimes encouragement needs words. Sometimes the best encouragement is just presence. Words can sometimes feel very superficial. On occasions it is a smile or a nod at the end of a conversation that provides just the right sort of encouragement. In these situations words would seem like mere platitudes and would detract from that sense of warmth and encouragement as the two people move into their next steps. A written card or note can also reinforce this encouragement very powerfully.

Seven principles for effective encouragement

In *The Art of Persuasion* Juliet Erickson identifies seven principles of effective communication that are particularly appropriate to encouraging conversations.

- **Forget rules**. Do not apply rigid rules and set speeches. Rely on awareness and flexibility: awareness both of the needs of the individual and of your own self-awareness; flexibility in terms of responding in whatever seems the most appropriate way.
- **Build rapport**. This puts building a quality relationship first.
- **Be yourself**. Cultivate the ability to feel natural and relaxed in any situation. When we fake who we are, the listener will sense something unreal. Being yourself does not mean making no effort or being sloppy. Being

yourself means being comfortable with yourself, at ease and natural – and that is not always very easy.

- **Focus on the individual**. The focus is not on you but on the other person. Real awareness in a conversation comes from knowing as much as you can about the situation of that other person.
- **Be definite**. Be firm in your encouragement, which allows you to speak about it with genuine conviction and clarity.
- **Actions speak loudest**. It is not just the words that are important, it is behaviour, appearance, gestures and unspoken empathy. The encouragement comes through who you are rather than through what you are actually saying.
- **Stay present**. Be aware of the moment you are in, and do not allow yourself to be lost in the past or the future.

Next steps

Having thought carefully about the nature of encouragement and its use in conversation, what can we now add to the themes we identified from Jesus' conversations at the start of the chapter?

- **Intimacy**. Are there more opportunities we could use to be one to one with individuals we could encourage? Could we take more opportunities at the end of meetings or gatherings, during the lunch break or in the evenings to spend some time being a source of encouragement for someone in our community? Jesus set the example of finding time and space to be with individuals.

- **Trust**. At the heart of successful encouraging conversations is trust. Trust can so easily be weakened without our being fully aware of the damage that is being done. It is worth checking regularly that trust is still there. Sometimes when trust has been eroded there needs to be honest conversation to ensure that the relationship gets back on the right track. If trust is undermined there will be a holding back in communication and a suspicion about the validity of encouraging remarks. Are there ways in which you can reinforce trust in conversations where you have a crucial role as an encourager?

- **Openness**. How willing are we to be open and to share from our experience in a way that will encourage others? Do we create an environment in which a friend or acquaintance would be willing to open up about some of their concerns?

- **Surprise**. Can we use surprise as a means of encouragement? It may be words of encouragement at unexpected moments. It could be a card, letter or bunch of flowers. People's needs are not run by clockwork: if we can be spontaneous in encouragement, we can play a powerful part in helping someone stay positive.

- **Understanding the context**. Can we deliberately set out to understand the context in which someone is living prior to a conversation? What are likely to be the pressures on them? Before I begin a coaching discussion I always spend the preceding five minutes in quiet reflection, imagining I am in the shoes of the person I am about to meet and trying to have a sensitivity about the emotions that will be going through their mind and heart as they come into this discussion. Often I cannot anticipate the particular context, but from previous contacts it does help enormously to try to imagine their emotions and their sensitivities at that time. I am quite certain that five minutes spent trying to picture the context before starting a discussion pays huge dividends. As you walk up to someone or as you see an acquaintance on the station platform, try to think what emotions are likely to be uppermost in their mind at that instant. Jesus so powerfully understood the context from which the Samaritan woman came.

- **Reassurance**. How can you help affirm someone? It may be through some positive words of praise or an expression of gratitude about a particular contribution they have made. Words of praise can be very powerful in setting the tone for an encouraging conversation. Done routinely it can appear a bit trite, but words of affirmation said with a sparkle in the eyes at the start of a conversation can set things off on the right track very effectively.

- **Stretching**. Good encouraging conversations are not just a slap on the back about the past. They are about stretching an individual's thinking and building on what has happened in the past. Good conversations need to keep moving forward so that there is not just a reassurance about the past but a development in new thinking for the future.

- **Sense of direction**. It is often helpful to think about where conversations are likely to be leading. This is not about forcing a conversation in a particular direction, but about considering some of the long-term outcomes that might result from encouraging conversations. Where an encouraging conversation is addressing a particular practical issue, it can be helpful to have in mind the next few steps that need to be taken.

- **Challenge**. When we encourage it can sometimes be right to challenge, to stimulate a change in action. Encouragement with a purpose will mean keeping ourselves and those we encourage 'on their toes'. Encouragement always needs to be unconditional, but sometimes the edge of challenge is an essential part of it. Jesus built challenge most effectively into his words of encouragement.

Questions for reflection

If this chapter has helped you think through some of the issues concerning encouragement, you might find the questions below to be useful prompts to further reflection and action.

1. If you had been the Samaritan woman or Thomas or Philip, how would you have felt encouraged by what Jesus said in conversation?
2. What aspect of Jesus' approach was most encouraging? How would you have responded to the challenging edge in his encouragement?
3. Who has had the most impact on you as an encourager?
4. How good are you at being encouraged by others?
5. Which groups of people or individuals can you have the biggest impact on as an encourager? How can you effectively both encourage and challenge them?
6. How might you take forward in encouraging conversations the practical themes of intimacy, openness, understanding the context, reassurance, stretching, sense of direction and challenge?

Challenging conversations 4

We all engage in challenging conversations. Sometimes they are challenging because they are difficult emotionally. Sometimes they are challenging because the person we are talking with has a very different point of view. Sometimes we try to avoid challenging conversations, only to regret it later. Challenging conversations often need careful preparation and a strong nerve, irrespective of which side of the conversation we are on. Sometimes they are challenging because we are nervous or we feel out of our depth.

We begin by looking at two very different sorts of challenging conversations. The first is between Jesus and Nicodemus and the second between Jesus and the Pharisees about the Sabbath.

> Now there was a man of the Pharisees named Nicodemus, a member of the Jewish ruling council. He came to Jesus at night and said, 'Rabbi, we know you are a teacher who has come from God. For no one could perform the miraculous signs you are doing if God were not with him.'
>
> In reply Jesus declared, 'I tell you the truth, no one can see the kingdom of God unless he is born again.'
>
> 'How can a man be born when he is old?' Nicodemus asked. 'Surely he cannot enter a second time into his mother's womb to be born!'

Jesus answered, 'I tell you the truth, no one can enter the kingdom of God unless he is born of water and the Spirit. Flesh gives birth to flesh, but the Spirit gives birth to spirit. You should not be surprised at my saying, "You must be born again." The wind blows wherever it pleases. You hear its sound, but you cannot tell where it comes from or where it is going. So it is with everyone born of the Spirit.'

'How can this be?' Nicodemus asked.

'You are Israel's teacher,' said Jesus, 'and do you not understand these things? I tell you the truth, we speak of what we know, and we testify to what we have seen, but still you people do not accept our testimony. I have spoken to you of earthly things and you do not believe; how then will you believe if I speak of heavenly things? No one has ever gone into heaven except the one who came from heaven – the Son of Man. Just as Moses lifted up the snake in the desert, so the Son of Man must be lifted up, that everyone who believes in him may have eternal life.

'For God so loved the world that he gave his one and only Son, that whoever believes in him shall not perish but have eternal life.' (Jn 3.1–16)

As a member of the Jewish ruling council, Nicodemus is a very senior figure in public life. He comes to see Jesus at night and affirms that Jesus is a teacher who has come from God. Jesus immediately makes the bold statement that no one can see the kingdom of God unless he is born again. As the conversation develops Jesus is very clear with Nicodemus: 'You must be born again.' When Nicodemus responds, 'How can this be?' Jesus persists in his challenge through references to the Old Testament and then through the clarity of his assertion that God so loved the world that he gave his only Son, 'that everyone who believes in him may have eternal life'. Jesus is relentless in his challenge to Nicodemus to stretch his thinking. He was not challenging Nicodemus without purpose: Nicodemus was clearly responding to the discussion and went on to become a strong supporter of Jesus.

The second example of a challenging conversation is rather different in tone. Jesus is talking with the Pharisees, who are attempting to undermine him and are not seeking to be stretched by a challenging conversation.

One Sabbath Jesus was going through the cornfields, and as his disciples walked along, they began to pick some ears of corn. The Pharisees said to him, 'Look, why are they doing what is unlawful on the Sabbath?'

He answered, 'Have you never read what David did when he and his companions were hungry and in need? In the days of Abiathar the high priest, he entered the house of God and ate the consecrated bread, which is lawful only for priests to eat. And he also gave some to his companions.'

Then he said to them, 'The Sabbath was made for man, not man for the Sabbath. So the Son of Man is Lord even of the Sabbath.'

Another time he went into the synagogue, and a man with a shrivelled hand was there. Some of them were looking for a reason to accuse Jesus, so they watched him closely to see if he would heal him on the Sabbath. Jesus said to the man with the shrivelled hand, 'Stand up in front of everyone.'

Then Jesus asked them, 'Which is lawful on the Sabbath: to do good or to do evil, to save life or to kill?' But they remained silent.

He looked around at them in anger and, deeply

distressed at their stubborn hearts, said to the man, 'Stretch out your hand.' He stretched it out, and his hand was completely restored. Then the Pharisees went out and began to plot with the Herodians how they might kill Jesus. (Mk 2.23–3.6)

Jesus listened to the challenge of the Pharisees and then responded clearly and memorably. He did not just dismiss the challenge, but quoted back relevant texts to the Pharisees and then offered them the pithy phrase, 'The Sabbath was made for man, not man for the Sabbath.' When the Pharisees challenged Jesus again, he put a question back to them: 'Which is lawful on the Sabbath: to do good or to do evil, to save life or to kill?' Responding to a question with a question silenced his critics.

At the end of the conversation there is an intriguing balance in Jesus' reaction, as he looked round at them in anger but was also deeply distressed at their stubborn hearts. Jesus was not to be put off by the Pharisees' challenge. He healed the man with the shrivelled hand, even though the result was that the Pharisees went out and began to plot how they might kill Jesus.

What key principles come out of these two stories?

- **Listen to understand**. Jesus listened to what the Pharisees had to say. He did not just ignore them. He heard them out before responding. He listened carefully to Nicodemus to understand where he was coming from.
- **Be clear**. Jesus gave full, clear answers in both challenging conversations. He did not shirk the issues.
- **Be memorable**. Jesus used very powerful pictorial phrases to illustrate his point – in particular 'being born

again' and 'the Sabbath was made for man, and not man for the Sabbath'.

- **Be bold and robust**. In both stories Jesus was bold: 'I tell you the truth.' You could say he was provocative in the way he asked the man with the withered hand to stand up in front of everyone.
- **Be persistent and focused**. Jesus did not let up in either of these conversations.
- **Be caring**. Jesus was never hard hearted. To Nicodemus he talked about God's love. With the Pharisees he was deeply distressed at their stubborn hearts.
- **Seek fuller understanding**. The heart of the challenge in both stories is that his hearers end up with a full rather than a partial understanding of what new life is about or what the Sabbath is for.
- **Use questions**. Jesus uses questions in a very direct, thoughtful way. He puts his hearers on the spot. They cannot avoid his questions. They are forced to think through their initial responses more clearly.

These principles are highly relevant for us as we encounter different sorts of challenging conversations. These might include difficult conversations at work with people who are taking a very different perspective from us, difficult negotiations, conversations within the workplace or the family where trust has broken down, conversations where you think the other person is completely wrong in their understanding or their actions and conversations where emotional tensions ride high and logic is not easy to embrace.

Examples of challenging conversations

Who have you had your most challenging conversations with? I remember various conversations in meetings with Tony Blair. He would listen carefully, but would then be very challenging with his questions and with his eyes. His approach was clear, focused and direct. I remember also a meeting between Basil Hume, the former Roman Catholic Archbishop of Westminster, and Mark Carlisle, who was then the Secretary of State for Education and Science. It was a difficult discussion about who would pay for school transport to Roman Catholic schools. The conversation was entirely good humoured, but the words were direct and strong. I was immensely impressed with Basil Hume's measured but resolute words, his eye contact and his firm sense of care for the young people under discussion.

As a teenager I can remember being challenged by an elderly neighbour. I used to visit her regularly when she was in her late 80s. She was a very independent lady coping admirably with ill health. Why did I as a teenager regularly go to see her? She had a very practical world view, she was full of determination and resolve, and she had an openness to local and national issues, a strong faith and a deep sense of practical compassion. Whenever we eat in our dining room now we sit on the dining chairs she used for 60 years, presented to her when her husband left his first curacy. These sturdy chairs are a reminder of the strong, searching questions she used to ask me in order to help me grow in my own understanding of my world and my faith.

Sometimes we can be challenging without realizing it. If we are abrupt or rather stony faced, we can give an impression of being rather more formidable than perhaps we want to be. Looking rather severe may simply be a sign of concentration, but we may need to correct that stance sometimes by ensuring that our face breaks into a smile, so that the challenge of the conversation is seen to be within a caring context.

Often when a challenging conversation is in prospect our knees begin to knock. Maybe there is a danger that we will not give of our best. A friend was going to see the chief executive of his organization. He was apprehensive. His Punjabi background meant that he was very deferential to authority. How would he approach the chief executive? What would he say?

I encouraged him to think of this discussion in a different way. The chief executive was very influential and a very significant player nationally. My friend was a middle manager, but one who had been marked out as having high potential. Could he think of the meeting as a conversation between equals? What was it that my friend was bringing to the party? He had information and insights about the way the organization was working and its impact on customers which would be invaluable to the chief executive. I knew the chief executive was a personable man and always welcoming. He would try to put my friend at ease. But how could I reassure my friend that this would be a good conversation?

I told him about the environment where they would meet. The chief executive did not have a formal table. He had a sofa and an easy chair. I encouraged my friend to think of himself in that environment, looking at the chief executive, smiling at him and sharing what was precious to him. I encouraged him to think about the things he was involved in that would be of interest to the chief executive. What could he share about his own experience? What did he want to share with the chief executive about his own learning and development? What could he ask the chief executive about his priorities for the region from which my friend came? What helpful insights could my friend offer? My final message was to think carefully about the broad topics he would like to have a conversation about and then to go into the discussion confident that it was going to be a valuable two-way exchange. I suggested that my friend should be as encouraging to the chief executive as he wanted him to be in return. He should shake his hand warmly, look him in the eye and smile.

One of the people I work with is brilliant at using challenging conversations as a crucial tool in his work. He spends his life having breakfast and dinner with key interlocutors. These discussions are one to one. He takes no acolytes with him and is very keen to meet people alone. He is always open, direct and frank. He uses hospitality thoughtfully. He is always welcoming. He sets the pace in discussion and is clear about what he would like to discuss. If a business partner is not delivering the goods, he is friendly but firm. If a supplier is not producing what he wants, he is straightforward and factual. He puts people on the spot, listens carefully and is frank about whether the response is adequate. The voice of challenge that he brings is not hostile, but it is unequivocal. He makes it absolutely clear that he wants to work together with the individual. He demonstrates the importance of a shared agenda and a shared understanding. He does not shrink from challenge.

People open up and tell him the difficulties that they would not necessarily want to share more widely. Over the bacon and scrambled egg he creates an opportunity for openness. This is not extravagant entertaining. He uses the context of a simple meal together to build a conversation in which issues can be addressed face to face and straight talking can lead to a clear set of action points. My friend is highly skilled at identifying the main issues and making certain they are on the table. You cannot escape a direct question given over a bowl of tomato soup, but at least taking another mouthful offers a moment to reflect and decide on the reply.

My friend's approach is never to be afraid to challenge, but always to do it in a safe environment where you are looking for positive outcomes. It is never challenge for the sake of challenge, or challenge to undermine. It is challenge that seeks to move an issue on and reach conclusions. No wonder my friend is hugely successful in taking change forward. He has built up the confidence of so many people so quickly. He challenges, but he is equally open to being challenged. He is willing to learn and change. The challenge process is not one way. The best of challengers seek out other people to challenge them and are ready to change their behaviour.

Media conversations

Journalists are very skilled at calling people to account. I recently read an interview in *The Times* with William Hague, the former leader of the Conservative Party in the UK, in which the interviewer asks if he believes in God. William Hague's response is, 'Yes, with a touch of agnosticism.' The journalist responds by saying that doesn't work. William Hague agrees. 'No, I don't know really. I'd like to, and I support the church out of believing in tradition and continuity, but I don't have strong religious beliefs of my own.'

The journalist responds, 'You're one of those Christians who likes the ethics but struggles with the spiritual side?'

William Hague says, 'That would be a good summary. I like and share the ethics but I'm not sure about the God bit.'

That is a challenging conversation at its best, in which the journalist presses William Hague to explain an obvious ambiguity and gives him the space to do so. William Hague is not beaten over the head in an aggressive way by the journalist, but the sequence of questions inevitably means that William Hague has to define what he means and then we, as readers, understand better what his position is. The journalist skilfully sums up his own understanding of William Hague's position and William Hague has no choice other than to say, 'That would be a good summary.' This interchange is a lovely example of how the most challenging conversations are not aggressive but involve a dialogue which defines truth ever more clearly.

Sharon is a highly effective TV interviewer. She looks at you warmly but intently. She describes successful TV interviews as requiring the interviewer to make the participant feel safe. That depends on the quality of preparation with the interviewee, however brief that may be. The topics for discussion need to be clear. The interviewer's role is to draw out the key points that the interviewee can contribute. But the sense of challenge must be there too. Once the interviewee feels safe and has responded on the initial territory, the interviewer can move into searching questions that may go beyond the original remit.

I spent two years as press secretary for Kenneth Baker and then John McGregor, who were both Secretaries of State for Education and Science. Preparation for interviews was crucial, with the key points being identified, shaped and refined. The best of interviewers would engage the Secretary of State and perhaps take the discussion further than had originally been intended. The most effective interviewers did challenge, but only after having established an initial basis of trust.

But is a media interview a conversation? I suspect that when I did TV and radio interviews as Government Regional Director in the north-east of England I could be rather staccato with prepared points in my mind. But there were occasions when a good interviewer helped to make my answers flow. In a strange way, when the interviewer challenged me in a structured way I became more coherent and perhaps more courageous. If the interviewer challenged me in a random and aggressive sort of way, I went straight back into my box with set answers.

It is sometimes interesting to observe a media interview to see how well or badly the interviewer asks questions. Is the interviewer listening to what the interviewee is saying? Are they building trust and demonstrating a sense of care? At the same time are they bold and robust as well as being persistent and focused in the interviewing? Reflecting on what went well or less well in a challenging conversation is a very positive way of reinforcing your own learning.

What do we do if we are challenged in conversation? How do we react? The principles introduced in this chapter are equally relevant if you are the one who is being challenged. Rather than reacting defensively or aggressively, it is worth taking a moment to listen and understand why somebody is taking that challenging approach. In these situations, viewing the conversation as a learning procedure in which we are trying to reinforce trust can help turn even the most difficult challenging conversation into a valuable experience. When somebody else has initiated a challenging conversation, we should not be inhibited from being firm in reply, once we have understood where they are coming from.

Writers on challenging conversations

Various writers have set out good advice on working through challenging conversations. Douglas Stone, Bruce Patton and Sheila Heen have written an excellent book called *Difficult Conversations*, following their work at the Harvard Negotiation Project. The heart of their approach is that when there is a difficult conversation, we should view it not as a 'message delivery stance' but as an opportunity for a 'learning conversation'. They see the starting point for difficult conversations as reducing your own fear and anxiety and entering into the conversation positively to see what you can learn from it. They set out a checklist for difficult conversations covering the following aspects.

- **Prepare**. Sort out what the facts are and what has happened so far. Understand your emotions, and be clear what is at stake for you in the conversation.
- **Check your purposes**. What do you hope to accomplish by having this conversation? What learning and problem-solving will result? Is this conversation the best way to address the issue and to achieve your purposes?
- **Start from the third story**. Describe the problem as the difference between two perspectives. Include both viewpoints as a legitimate part of the discussion and invite the other party to join in sorting out the situation together. As far as possible this turns a challenging conversation into a problem-solving conversation. The writers see curiosity as an important way into a challenging conversation. When you are very certain about your position, a strong sense of curiosity about why someone else is taking a different perspective can

provide very helpful new understanding about why that is. Curiosity can help you get inside someone's story so that you can better understand their stance. Curiosity is about learning someone's story, sharing your story and then, if possible, finding a way forward together. They advocate speaking for yourself with clarity and power in challenging situations. Their advice is to speak out the heart of the matter.

- **Start with what matters most**. Have you said what is at the heart of the matter for you? Have you shared what is at stake? If not, ask yourself why, and see if you can find the courage to try.
- **Say what you mean**. Don't make them guess. Don't rely on the subtext.
- **Don't make your story simplistic**. Be ready to include both positive and negative aspects so that your story has a reasonable balance within it.

Every challenging conversation is different. The focus on careful preparation and learning from the story of others is crucial. If challenging conversations can be viewed as learning conversations, we will be ready to be both firm in our views and willing to learn in the content of our perspective and also in our approach to such conversations.

Ann Dickson has written a book with the same title, *Difficult Conversations*. She describes a range of difficult conversations that frequently occur in intimate social and work situations and sets out techniques that can help to transform the situation. She concludes with ten valuable tips for difficult conversations.

1. Don't attempt to enter a conversation when you are experiencing any extreme emotion – shock, grief, fear, rage. Wait until you have achieved some distance from

the situation and your emotional level has diminished to a manageable level.

2. Never begin without your answer to the question, 'What specifically do I want to be different?' Have what you'd like clearly in mind beforehand.
3. Don't wait to tackle a problem until it happens again: take the initiative.
4. Don't initiate an important conversation while eating, drinking, making love, watching TV: always make a separate space and time to talk.
5. Don't initiate your discussion when you bump into someone in the corridor/shop/street. Arrange to meet beforehand.
6. Never bring in others to back up your opinion as extra leverage: confine yourself to your own feelings and views.
7. Don't let it go on and on: once you've said what you want to say and it has been heard, close.
8. Don't pile on one criticism after another '... and another thing ...' Keep to one item at a time.
9. Keep off the moral high ground: remember to take responsibility when necessary (usually) and keep it equal.
10. Don't 'ask for the impossible': ask for something that the other person is capable of changing.

Ann Dickson talks very powerfully of criticism, handled properly, as a real gift.

It's a gift because someone cares enough to make the effort to actually say something to me. This means to me that our relationship matters enough. When we take the risk of communicating difficult things, it means the other person matters – it means that living with, working with, being with this person matters enough for you to open up and speak your mind. The enrichment that can come from a renewed under-standing between people is surprising but inevitable.

Jenni Trent Hughes' book *Tough Talk Made Easy* discusses a whole range of challenging conversations covering family, friends, relationships, work and difficult con-frontations. When entering challenging conversations, she advises keeping in mind the purpose of the conversation: what do we want the results of the conversation to be? She also reminds us that once we've said it we can't take it back again.

In challenging conversations listening is even more important. She advises that when you are listening you should make the other person the absolute centre of your focus. Put everything else to one side until they have finished speaking. If you keep interrupting while a person is speaking, they will have the impression (quite correctly) that you are not listening. If you are thinking of what to say next, then that means you are not listening. Listen carefully to what the other person is saying and take it on board. Keep an eye also on the body language of the person you are talking to. If they are sitting with their arms folded, looking away from you, the chances are they are not listening. If you feel up to it, this is a good point to ask, 'Are you OK with this so far?' If you are not comfortable doing that, just slow down or stop and give them a chance to respond.

Next steps

How can we apply the principles we outlined earlier in the chapter to our own conversations?

- **Listen to understand**. Take a moment to reflect on why somebody is taking such a challenging approach before coming in with your own perceptions.
- **Be clear**. When you challenge, ask yourself if you are always as clear as you should be. Have you thought out in advance the key points that you want to make and the purpose of the conversation?
- **Be memorable**. Identify key phrases or stories that you want to bring into the conversation. If it is a challenging conversation about somebody's performance, have ready clear examples and pictures to illustrate what you want to say.
- **Be bold and robust**. Be clear about the facts and the key points you want to get across. Check whether your arguments stand up. Be ready to respond positively to the supplementary questions you are likely to be asked.
- **Be persistent and focused**. Enter the conversation with enough energy to carry your points through. Prepare supplementary points to underline the key theme that you want to put forward.
- **Be caring**. Uphold the other person as someone whose welfare you care about, however difficult they are being.
- **Seek fuller understanding**. Determine to continue to learn so that as a result of a challenging conversation your perspective grows and develops rather than becoming more rigid.
- **Use questions**. It might help to prepare questions in advance, both to help your confidence and to make

sure you are ready for the different ways the conversation might progress.

Questions for reflection

1. What are the most impressive things for you in the way Jesus took forward two very different types of challenging conversations?
2. What are the most challenging conversations in which you have been involved?
3. What is the best way for you to prepare for challenging conversations?
4. What sort of challenging conversations are likely to take place for you within the next few weeks? These could be in your family, your community, your church or your workplace.
5. How can you best prepare for challenging conversations?
6. How helpful is it for you to view a challenging conversation as a learning conversation?
7. How can you cope better with being challenged in conversation?
8. Can you think of some ways in which you might develop the principles from this chapter in your own conversations?

Short conversations

5

We spend our lives having short conversations with a wide range of people. Can you reflect on the different short conversations you have had today within your family, walking along the street, or with people in shops or at work? Have those conversations been purely functional, or have they been enjoyable? Can a conversation be functional and enjoyable at the same time?

Sometimes we make our short conversations as businesslike and as short as possible. On other occasions we use them as an opportunity to bring good cheer and encouragement to others. Like any type of conversation, it is not just about the words we use: our smile and tone of voice matter too. To put this into action effectively and consistently takes a lot of effort, but is well worth doing. Ticket collectors at busy stations, for example, are focusing on the tickets and not particularly looking at the passengers. But a cheerful 'good morning' and a smile can lift the eyes of that person and produce an answering smile, lifting the spirits of both you and the ticket collector.

There are frequent examples of short conversations in the life of Jesus. Our first conversation is the one Jesus had with Zacchaeus, the tax collector.

Jesus entered Jericho and was passing through. A man was there by the name of Zacchaeus; he was a chief tax collector and was wealthy. He wanted to see who Jesus was, but being a short man he could not, because of the crowd. So he ran ahead and climbed a sycamore-fig tree to see him, since Jesus was coming that way.

When Jesus reached the spot, he looked up and said to him, 'Zacchaeus, come down immediately. I must stay at your house today.' So he came down at once and welcomed him gladly.

All the people saw this and began to mutter, 'He has gone to be the guest of a "sinner".'

But Zacchaeus stood up and said to the Lord, 'Look, Lord! Here and now I give half of my possessions to the poor, and if I have cheated anybody out of anything, I will pay back four times the amount.'

Jesus said to him, 'Today salvation has come to this house, because this man, too, is a son of Abraham. For the Son of Man came to seek and to save what was lost.' (Lk. 19.1–10)

The initial conversation between Jesus and Zacchaeus is very short. Jesus looks up and sees Zacchaeus in a tree and says, 'Zacchaeus, come down immediately. I must stay at your house today.' Zacchaeus responds straight away and welcomes Jesus gladly into his home. Later on there is another brief conversation when Zacchaeus declares that he is going to give half his possessions to the poor and will pay back four times the amount owed to those people he has cheated. Jesus responds briefly about the Son of Man coming to seek and save what was lost.

In these short conversations Jesus was clear, brief and positive. He took risks and asked to visit the house of someone who was unpopular. As a result the crowds muttered that he had gone to be 'the guest of a sinner'. Jesus was very clear on the impact of the short conversation. After Zacchaeus declared his intention to pay back the money he owed, there was no long sermon from Jesus, just a brief couple of sentences about it being a special day. Jesus did not need to use many words, because the few words from Zacchaeus summed up all that needed to be said.

The impact of Jesus' words came through their brevity and their perceptiveness. Jesus had spotted Zacchaeus in the tree. Maybe he knew some of the background to his unpopularity as a tax collector. The short conversation did not start with concerns about his financial dealings: it was all about identifying with Zacchaeus. The initial conversation – 'I must stay at your house today' – was purely about hospitality. It then led on to a wonderful confession and a practical resolution for the future.

The second example of a short conversation is the exchange Jesus had with the blind man at Bethsaida.

> They came to Bethsaida, and some people brought a blind man and begged Jesus to touch him. He took the blind man by the hand and led him outside the village. When he had spat on the man's eyes and put his hands on him, Jesus asked, 'Do you see anything?'
>
> He looked up and said, 'I see people; they look like trees walking around.'
>
> Once more Jesus put his hands on the man's eyes. Then his eyes were opened, his sight was restored, and he saw everything clearly. Jesus sent him home, saying, 'Don't go into the village.' (Mk 8.22–26)

There are many examples of Jesus having short conversations with people who needed healing. This short story has some wonderful touches in it. It may be a summary of a longer conversation, but the passage certainly brings out the heart of the exchange. When Jesus met the blind man, his first response was to take him by the hand and lead him outside the village. His first act was not to heal the blind man, but to walk alongside him. After Jesus had put his hands on the blind man he just said to him, 'Do you see anything?' After the blind man talked of seeing people looking like trees walking around, Jesus put his hands on the man's eyes again. Then his eyes were opened and his sight restored. Once the man was healed Jesus gave the very brief injunction, 'Don't go into the village.'

What is so characteristic of Jesus in this story is the physical act of support: he led the man by the hand and touched his eyes. He asked one short, factual question and then sent the healed man away quietly so that he did not go into the village. Jesus did not want to draw attention to himself or create embarrassment for the man, for he would surely have become the centre of attention had he gone immediately back into the village.

What practical messages can we take from these two short conversations?

- **Be alongside**. Jesus wanted to visit the house of Zacchaeus; he led the blind man by the hand. He was present, connecting personally with both individuals.
- **Spot the key issue**. Jesus knew precisely how to speak to Zacchaeus in a very personal way. 'I must stay at your home today.' He went straight to the heart of the matter. The focus with the blind man was purely on bringing healing.
- **Be clear**. Jesus did not mince his words. He said to Zacchaeus, 'Come down immediately,' and to the blind man, 'Do you see anything?'

- **Don't waste words**. The recorded comments of Jesus could hardly have been briefer. That brevity enhanced the power of what he said.
- **Take risks**. Asking to visit the home of the unpopular tax collector was not going to endear Jesus to certain members of the crowd. He healed the blind man even though he knew this would be controversial.
- **Be purposeful**. Jesus' short conversations were not just about passing the time of day, but spoke to the needs of the individuals in a very powerful way.
- **Be self-effacing**. In the story of Zacchaeus the punchline comes from Zacchaeus, and not from Jesus, when he says that he will pay back four times his debt. The positive outcome of the short conversation is not what Jesus does but what Zacchaeus says. The success of the short conversation is in the action of Zacchaeus: he is the star in this conversation, with Jesus as a very crucial prompt. With the blind man Jesus does not draw attention to himself and encourages the healed man not to go back into the village at that point.
- **Short conversations can lead to significant conclusions**. The initial conversation with Zacchaeus was purely about visiting his house. The ultimate outcome was much more dramatic. It is not clear whether Jesus anticipated the eventual outcome, but he embarked on a short conversation in a way which had the potential of leading to something more significant. The brief conversation with the blind man at Bethsaida became part of Mark's Gospel and has had a significant impact over 2,000 years.

We engage in many different types of short conversations every day. What follows is a range of examples in which these simple principles are just as relevant.

Memorable short conversations

I think that the most depressing short conversations I ever had took place when, for a couple of hours, I acted as a messenger delivering the mail within an organization where I worked. I was a Board Member in an organization employing 5,000 people. We decided that we should see what it was like to experience different jobs within that organization. I delivered the mail in a part of the organization where I was not well known. I donned the uniform and began to do the job in a cheerful frame of mind. I rapidly discovered that the in-trays were in a variety of awkward places. People working in the offices either ignored me or grunted at me. Nobody smiled or passed the time of day. I definitely felt like the lowest of the low. I wanted to be cheerful, but was met by surly expressions. I tried to start some conversations, but received only silence or one-word answers in return. It was a very salutary experience to be the recipient of such a blank wall of silence. I resolved that never again would I ignore those wonderful people providing services so essential for our existence.

Last Christmas my family decided that, rather than having Christmas Day at home, we would help run the local Christmas Day Lunch for people who would otherwise eat alone. Initially I had no enthusiasm for this. Did I really want to spend Christmas Day in a church hall talking with about 60 people I did not know? It turned out to be a wonderful day full of fascinating short conversations. In some of them there were few words. Some of the people were clearly mentally challenged. One guest rather aggressively demanded to know each of the helpers' birthdays and proudly told us what day of the week our birthdays would fall on in the next year. Someone else wanted a cup of tea every 15 minutes. The fact that someone else was providing that tea meant it was such an important repeated conversation for her. George had shoed horses for 57 years. He proudly told me he had never ridden a horse but he could talk to horses, who liked silence. The horses recognized him each time he came, and he had wonderful conversations with them to calm them down. Sam, aged 93, shared with me that his wife and his daughter had died, but he was still positive about life. He talked with tears of joy in his eyes about his grandchildren and great-grandchildren. Mabel proudly told me that she was 98½ and very keen to reach the age of 100. She said that she kept being asked to do things at church, which was just what she wanted. Sadly, one lady rather plaintively said, 'I'm OK, but I had hoped my daughter would have been in touch with me this year.' Holding her hand at that point was what was needed, rather than words.

A couple I drove to the lunch shuffled from the house to the car and did not find the travelling or the conversation easy. They sat peacefully together, however, and exchanged brief words and glowed as the afternoon went on, glad to be singing carols as part of a wider community. There was a peacefulness and pleasure in their eyes at not being alone, even though they exchanged few words with others who were present.

At the end of that Christmas Day I hoped that we had brought good cheer to these folk. But it was what they gave me that took me aback. As they shared some of their stories with me I felt grateful to them for their steadfastness and their courage. Although all these conversations were short, the practical lessons were relevant to a wide range of conversations. It was all about the privilege of listening and being willing to put energy into conversations with people whose responsiveness varied.

Doctors' conversations

Doctors never stop having short conversations. Chris Jagger is a friend who works both as a GP and as a hospital doctor. He writes,

> Short, encouraging conversations in the workplace can be very helpful indeed. Saying 'Well done' to someone for a job done or 'Thank you' to the staff at the end of the day is important. The practice of surgeons saying 'Thank you' to the Head Operating Sister at the end of each operation is crucial. Swing-door conversations receive a bad press, but in my view even the briefest of conversations during the day can have an enormous value especially if accompanied by a smile. I try and make an effort to speak to the cleaners in the hospital and all echelons of the nursing team. A cheerful 'Hello' can alter the way people feel about themselves.

Another doctor told me of the emotions she went through when meeting each patient in the surgery. She had such a short period to weigh up the right decision about treatment. She said that she listened to their words and watched their eyes and body language. Were they telling the whole truth or just certain aspects of the truth? How much pain were they really in? In that short conversation she was drawing on her factual understanding but also her intuition in order to understand and then take purposeful action. She had to reach judgements and stretch her understanding. The conclusions would not necessarily be right all the time, but she had to decide very quickly what she should do next in the light of all the signals she was getting from the patient. No wonder she was completely drained after each surgery session. She said that she was forever learning how to read people better and use those short conversations to the best possible effect. I asked her what really made the difference. She said the key was to watch, listen and ask the right questions.

When you walk in the room

How often have you been daunted by the act of entering a large room full of people? Who do you talk to first? What is the purpose of these conversations? For a period I worked closely with Lord Dearing, who was formerly Chief Executive of the Post Office in the UK and chaired various senior committees on education reform. When he was Chair of the Northern Development Company, he used to visit the region one day a week. He was always in the north-east for key events and could work a room fantastically. He kept full eye contact with each individual. He was completely engrossed in their 'story' for the time he was talking with them. He would then discreetly move on to talk to someone else after two or three minutes. In the period that an individual was talking to him, he or she had his sole and undivided attention. People opened up with him and told him things that they would not necessarily have planned to say. He possessed a great gift to draw people out of themselves in a very short space of time.

In her book *The Art of Persuasion* Juliet Erickson talks of the following steps in the context of such short conversations.

- When you walk into a room, leave your baggage outside the door. There is nothing else. Only that moment.

- Believe that there is something interesting in everyone and look for it.
- Believe that you have something each person can benefit from, namely your energy and interest.
- Give as much good as you can to each person. This does not mean walking around blessing each person and anointing them with oil. At least, not overtly – just with your intent.

Learning from experience

For those with children life can be very full of short conversations. Research has been done using microphones on children, and sadly the amount of time spent in conversation with fathers is often less than one minute per day. The message from my doctor friend, Chris Jagger, was, 'This is humbling for all of us. These regular short conversations with children need to have certain elements, including reassuring, encouraging, warning against dangers, inspiring, loving, enfolding, challenging and, most important of all, listening and valuing.'

Have you ever had short conversations in which you have not been as even tempered as you wanted to be? Have you then regretted your sharp words? Recently I was told by someone at the railway station ticket office that I would not be eligible for a 5 per cent discount on the renewal of my annual season ticket because I was adding a tube journey to the cost of the rail ticket. I thought this was very unfair and became rather abrupt with the individual selling tickets. She patiently gave me the telephone number of the customer relations officer. I stomped off and phoned this number, not in the coolest frame of mind. The person I spoke to could not have been more helpful. She was about to go home, but turned her computer back on and provided me with an answer that I thought was fair and right. The fact that she showed such cheerfulness and helpfulness put me to shame. The individual at the ticket office was only doing her job according to the clear brief she had been given. I had been wrong to snap at her. I have been so much better at being patient with transport staff since then. The lady on the phone was called Georgina, and I have tried to keep in mind her helpful and friendly tone of voice. It made all the difference that day.

We all have stories like this. Holding in our minds the faces or voices of people who have been particularly helpful in short conversations when we have been showing some signs of impatience is a wonderful way of ensuring more measured behaviour on future occasions. The voice of Georgina from South West Trains is a still small voice, or rather a very cheerful, helpful voice, ringing in my ears. Are there similar voices that you may find helpful to remember?

The most memorable short conversation I ever had was with Her Majesty the Queen when I received my CB (the rather bizarre title of Companion of the Order of the Bath). The Queen put the medal over my head and onto my shoulders and then asked me a couple of questions. I knew from previous recipients that the Queen would ask two questions. The length of my audience would depend on how long and interesting my replies were. I was ready with my answers. While I spoke, the Queen's eyes were completely focused on me and I felt that she was fully absorbed in those moments, in my answers and in who I was. That morning the Queen spoke with the same degree of intensity to 100 people. The powerful way in which she listened to someone she had never met before and would almost certainly never meet again was a revelation. If the Queen could give me her sole and undivided attention for that one minute, then surely I must try to do the same with the people I meet, however briefly.

The town where I live has a special relationship with Georgia in the USA, as the first governor of Georgia was originally a resident of Godalming. We recently entertained some American visitors from Georgia. We knew that the conversations would be brief and that we were unlikely to see these people again. But we discovered a richness of common heritage. We found much to share and laugh about and we went away feeling like good friends. We did not just stay on a superficial level. We talked about matters of faith and practical aspects of retirement. The conversations were purposeful, enjoyable and encouraging. Sometimes we think that short conversations are inevitably going to be superficial, but that need not be the case. The conversations with our American visitors were short but rich. We searched for what was important to our guests and led them towards places that were special to them. The shortness did not matter, it was the depth that was so valuable.

Short conversations as an adventure

Can I encourage you to think of each day as an adventure into a sequence of short conversations? You might like to note down at the end of a day the short conversations you have had and some of the points you have learnt from them.

As a stimulus, I would like to share with you one recent

Monday which was full of short conversations. I had to get an early flight from London to Edinburgh, leaving home at 5 a.m. After five minutes on the road I noticed there was virtually no fuel in the car. My immediate and grumpy thought was, 'Who used the car last?' What a relief to find a petrol station open 24 hours a day and to have a cheerful conversation with the man on the till, who said he thoroughly enjoyed working nights. A lady at the airport gave me helpful advice about how to use the automatic check-in arrangements. Learning something new at six o'clock on a Monday morning was quite exciting. The air hostesses were bright and cheerful in our brief exchanges, which helped me prepare for a busy day. In Edinburgh the bus driver was very clear with his instructions about the route through Charlotte Square. He did not seem to mind me talking to him as he drove slowly through the busy traffic.

At my destination the secretary, Linda, gave me a big welcome with hot coffee and chocolate biscuits. I talked to a personnel manager about going to a difficult meeting with people who were turning to personal criticism. We talked about being true to oneself and doing what you thought was right in difficult situations. Between three lengthy coaching discussions in different contexts, two receptionists brightened my day with their smiles and cheerful voices, and three taxi drivers were efficient and delightful, telling me about the pleasures of working in Edinburgh.

On the way back, at the airport, a very grumpy assistant did not seem particularly willing to sell me a coffee and a biscuit. Perhaps this was my comeuppance for wanting a biscuit with my coffee! I isolated myself in the departure lounge, curled up with a dictating machine recording the key points of that day's coaching discussions. Then I got into trouble with the lady on the departure gate for not having heard the call for my flight until the last minute.

The most interesting discussion of the day was with the chief flight attendant, who told me about the range of short conversations she had. The confines of an aircraft with no space and lots of alcohol are a recipe for grumpiness and potential difficulty. The flight attendants are trained to be cheerful. Veronica said they always look people in the eye and smile: it makes such a difference. If people smile back at them that makes the attendants feel good and want to serve them even better. She was full of stories of short conversations with members of famous football teams and leading politicians. What mattered was not who they were but what sort of tone they had adopted: had they smiled, had they been cheerful, had they said 'thank you'? She said that sometimes the flight attendants had to look rather fierce when people failed to put their seats back up or fasten their seat belts. Part of the fun was deciding when to be cheerful and when to be a bit fierce.

Veronica told me that the great variety of short conversations she had as a flight attendant meant that she enjoyed any chance of repartee with new and different people. It even meant that one of her pleasures in life was speed dating where four minutes of brief conversation was, she thought, such a good way of seeing whether a man had any charm or even depth. She said that in just four minutes you can weigh somebody up and know whether you are going to get on with them.

My day in Edinburgh included some non-conversations. The airport bus at 5.45 a.m. was full of dour besuited gents. A bright word, or even a cheerful look, would have felt totally out of place. My companions on the morning flight in their smart Monday shirts and deep blue ties were engrossed in their newspapers and even the British Airways breakfast, but there was no danger that they were going to be engrossed in conversation. Walking down Princes Street on a cold, frosty morning, everyone was purposeful rather than engaging. The exception was an American lady who asked me the way. I had to admit that I was a visitor too. 'That's fine,' she said, making full allowance for my inadequacies. Perhaps that was the best short conversation of the day, because she did not mind that we failed to communicate in the way she had hoped.

Be ready to be surprised

As an example of surprising short conversations, let me tell you about a friend who wrote saying that his view of prostitutes had 'completely changed'. As he was only 19, we wondered what had brought on this dramatic change of view. He had been on a Christian mission with some other young people in a city where they had given roses to prostitutes. One girl had talked with them brightly and openly, saying that she had a young family and this was her means of raising income. She was very responsive to their questions. They were shocked, surprised and troubled by her story, but felt respect for her at the same time. That was a highly responsive sort of conversation, which left them very thoughtful about the circumstances in which this lady had found herself, locked into a situation from which she could not escape.

Perhaps for me the most special short conversation was with a teenager who had a reputation for violent behaviour. A personal adviser working with young people in difficult circumstances had taken a particular interest in him and encouraged his interest in fishing. This troubled young man shared with me the joy he found in fishing. His eyes lit up as he talked about his hobby. This gave me great pleasure. The greatest pleasure, however, was in seeing how much the personal adviser had achieved by persevering in conversation with this young man. By encouraging him to pursue his hobby of fishing, the adviser had helped to dissipate the anger that youngster felt in himself and the acts of violence were now a thing of the past. The short conversation I had with that young man was special because it uplifted me.

Next steps

Against the background of these different examples of short conversations, we return to the themes we picked out from Jesus' conversations. How can we take these on board as practical guidelines for ourselves?

- **Be alongside**. Sometimes a smile, a handshake, or even a hug can be a very powerful signal that we are alongside someone when there is only an opportunity for a very brief conversation. For example, a bereaved person needs a handshake or hug and not a deluge of words.
- **Spot the key issue**. This is about reflecting on what could be the most valuable use of the brief time you are going to spend with someone. Think yourself into their shoes so that you can open up a brief flow of conversation that will be as helpful as possible to them.
- **Be clear**. When we see a need, sometimes we can be direct in asking if we can help. It can be as simple as offering a proper 'thank you' to a shopkeeper or ticket

collector – and doing it with a smile so it is clear that the gesture is genuine.

- **Don't waste words**. Sometimes we can be more direct than we generally think is legitimate. Sometimes we hide our perceptions when it would be better to be quite explicit. If we ask directly whether a particular issue is troubling somebody, we may enable a short but fruitful conversation to take place. Jesus went straight to the point with Zacchaeus: the change of heart from the tax collector followed a few steps later on.

- **Take risks**. Sometimes we need to be bold and start conversations with people who do not look as if they want to be engaged. Sometimes it is right to keep one's distance, but on other occasions taking the first step in conversation is crucial in order to help someone who looks despondent.

- **Be purposeful**. Think ahead constructively about how to use short conversations in a positive way. Sometimes it helps to plan what you are going to say to people you meet briefly.

- **Be self-effacing**. Short conversations succeed when the questioner focuses on the interests of the person to whom they are speaking. Reflecting that person's interests and building up their self-esteem is where a good short conversation often starts.

- **Short conversations can lead to significant conclusions**. Short conversations have a value in themselves, but they can lead to surprising results. If we go into short conversations with the anticipation that some of them will lead into new insights or surprises, then we will view such conversations with natural curiosity. Allowing that natural curiosity freedom while not impinging on an individual's privacy is a delicate balancing act.

Short conversations are not just exchanges that we initiate. We are recipients too. The principles above apply just as much in those cases. We will gain most out of short conversations as recipients when we are ready to respond and are open to new events and people.

Questions for reflection

1. Are there particular applications you can draw from the stories of Jesus talking to Zacchaeus and the blind man?
2. What are the most memorable short conversations that you have had?
3. In what ways would you like to use short conversations differently in the future?
4. How might you be surprised by the outcomes of short conversations?
5. How might you apply some of the principles illustrated in this chapter?

Painful conversations

6

Some conversations are not straightforward and can be very painful. We sometimes avoid painful conversations and try to rationalize why we cannot participate in them. On other occasions there is no avoiding the task of giving somebody painful news. Painful conversations come in many different shapes and sizes. Some are self-inflicted, others are just facts of life. How we move on from painful conversations is often a test of great courage. For some it is part of their job to be involved in painful conversations. The ability to move on in those circumstances becomes all the more important. Painful conversations can include a surprising amount of humour. They can be remarkably healing. The first step is often the most difficult one.

The illustrations from the life of Jesus involve two very different sorts of painful conversations. The first is with the rich young ruler.

As Jesus started on his way, a man ran up to him and fell on his knees before him. 'Good teacher,' he asked, 'what must I do to inherit eternal life?'

'Why do you call me good?' Jesus answered. 'No one is good – except God alone. You know the commandments: "Do not murder, do not commit adultery, do not steal, do not give false testimony, do not defraud, honour your father and mother."'

'Teacher,' he declared, 'all these I have kept since I was a boy.'

Jesus looked at him and loved him. 'One thing you lack,' he said. 'Go, sell everything you have and give to the poor, and you will have treasure in heaven. Then come, follow me.'

At this the man's face fell. He went away sad, because he had great wealth.

Jesus looked around and said to his disciples, 'How hard it is for the rich to enter the kingdom of God!'

The disciples were amazed at his words. But Jesus said again, 'Children, how hard it is to enter the kingdom of God! It is easier for a camel to go through the eye of a needle than for a rich man to enter the kingdom of God.'

The disciples were even more amazed, and said to each other, 'Who then can be saved?'

Jesus looked at them and said, 'With man this is impossible, but not with God; all things are possible with God.'

Peter said to him, 'We have left everything to follow you!'

'I tell you the truth,' Jesus replied, 'no one who has left home or brothers or sisters or mother or father or children or fields for me and the gospel will fail to receive a hundred times as much in this present age (homes, brothers, sisters, mothers, children and fields – and with them, persecutions) and in the age to come, eternal life. But many who are first will be last, and the last first.' (Mk 10.17–31)

The rich young ruler comes earnestly to Jesus, falls on his knees and asks what he must do to inherit eternal life. Jesus asks if he has followed the ten commandments, to which the young man readily responds. Jesus then goes to the heart of the man's preoccupation with wealth and challenges him to go and sell everything he has and give to the poor. The man's face falls and he goes away sad. The conversation was painful for the rich young ruler because he felt unable to give his wealth away. It was painful for Jesus to see the man's enthusiasm dissipate.

The conversation that follows between Jesus and Peter is equally painful. Jesus talks about it being easier for a camel to go through the eye of a needle than for a rich man to enter the kingdom of God. The conversation is then at cross purposes, with Jesus talking about what is impossible with man but possible with God and Peter talking about the disciples having left everything to follow Jesus. In these conversations where the disciples are showing partial understanding, there must have been pain for Jesus in having to come to terms with the prospect of his death on his own. The key to this story is the phrase, 'With man this is impossible, but not with God; all things are possible with God.' Jesus makes the disciples face up to difficult issues, but he offers hope and encouragement and challenges them to raise their sights.

The second passage is a sequence of painful conversations shortly before Jesus' death.

> They went to a place called Gethsemane, and Jesus said to his disciples, 'Sit here while I pray.' He took Peter, James and John along with him, and he began to be deeply distressed and troubled. 'My soul is overwhelmed with sorrow to the point of death,' he said to them. 'Stay here and keep watch.'
>
> Going a little farther, he fell to the ground and prayed that if possible the hour might pass from him. '*Abba*, Father,' he said, 'everything is possible for you. Take

this cup from me. Yet not what I will, but what you will.'

Then he returned to his disciples and found them sleeping. 'Simon,' he said to Peter, 'are you asleep? Could you not keep watch for one hour? Watch and pray so that you will not fall into temptation. The spirit is willing, but the body is weak.'

Once more he went away and prayed the same thing. When he came back, he again found them sleeping, because their eyes were heavy. They did not know what to say to him.

Returning the third time, he said to them, 'Are you still sleeping and resting? Enough! The hour has come. Look, the Son of Man is betrayed into the hands of sinners. Rise! Let us go! Here comes my betrayer!' (Mk 14.32–42)

While at Gethsemane Jesus' heart is troubled and he is overwhelmed with sorrow. He asks the three disciples to stay and keep watch, but when he returns he finds them sleeping. He says, 'Could you not keep watch for one hour?' For a second time he asks them to watch and pray, but when he returns they are sleeping because their eyes are heavy. They are embarrassed and do not know what to say to him. When he returns a third time he asks, 'Are you still sleeping and resting?' Then he says, 'The hour has come ... here comes my betrayer.'

In the midst of the painful series of conversations with the disciples there is a painful conversation with God. Jesus falls to the ground and asks that, if possible, the hour might pass from him. During that conversation he accepts the inevitable – that he should be crucified. At the end of these painful conversations Jesus says, 'Rise! Let us go!'

The key themes we can take from these stories are as follows:

- **Start with understanding**. Jesus listened to the rich young ruler, understood where he was coming from and did not dismiss his enthusiasm. He understood the tiredness of the three disciples, even though he was exasperated by their inability to continue in prayer.
- **Be focused**. Jesus went to the heart of the matter with the rich young ruler in terms of pinpointing his concern for material wealth. Jesus at Gethsemane was focused in his need for quietness and prayer as well as in his concern that the disciples could not stay awake.
- **Be consistent**. As Jesus talked to the rich young ruler and then to the disciples he was consistent in his message about the importance of giving up material wealth. He showed the same consistency in his request for the three disciples to stay awake and keep watch.
- **Be sensitive to your own emotions**. Jesus did not hide the emotions he was feeling in Gethsemane when wrestling with his own destiny. He was exasperated with the disciples.
- **Share pain**. Jesus was downcast that the rich young ruler went away sad. He shared in his pain. He commented on how hard it is for the rich to enter the kingdom of God. At Gethsemane he felt sadness that the disciples could not share in his pain, as they kept falling asleep rather than watching and praying.
- **Leave space**. Jesus gave the rich young man space to talk through what was on his heart. He created space in Gethsemane to be alone and then to be together with the three disciples who were closest to him. He wanted their support at a painful time.

- **Move on**. After the rich young ruler had gone away sad, Jesus used the memorable phrase, 'how hard it is for the rich to enter the kingdom of God', to demonstrate the necessity of giving up certain things that seem important at the time. In Gethsemane, even though the disciples kept falling asleep, he wanted them with him. He said, 'Let *us* go.'
- **Offer continuing support**. As Jesus went to meet his betrayer, his words, 'Rise! Let us go!' showed his continuing support for his disciples. He was still building them up and asking them to be with him, even though they were learning slowly.

Painful conversations with children and young people

In each of our personal histories there will have been painful conversations. I can still vividly remember the day my mother sat me, aged 7, on her knee and told me that my father had died of a heart attack. It took time for that devastating news to sink in. I lost my confidence for a number of years. My mother initiated that painful conversation with care and thoughtfulness. It would have been equally painful for her. For the rest of my childhood I wanted to do my best for my dad.

Painful conversations with children last in their minds for ever. Preparing carefully for these conversations and taking them forward in a relaxed and yet purposeful way is crucial. Painful messages delivered badly to children can leave long-term scars.

The pain of humiliation in conversation is equally significant in the teenage years. Youngsters in this age group may well be very difficult to communicate with. But painful messages will be just as difficult to receive. The 16-year-old full of bravado will feel just as much pain as a 6-year-old or a 26-year-old, but will attempt to hide it in a very different way. Painful conversations are perhaps hardest to have with teenagers when the emotional understanding of a child is still contained within the physical appearance of a near-adult.

In a society where fewer marriages survive, there are perhaps many more painful conversations between children and parents. Under the title of 'Modern Times', the *Daily Mail* had an article by Kathryn Knight (23 December 2004) about painful conversations at Christmas. Laura, a 17-year-old, has a crumpled but treasured family photograph of herself as a toddler with smiling parents and grandparents. The picture is a happy festive memento but also a bittersweet one, as her parents separated shortly afterwards. Now studying for A levels, Laura tells the journalist, 'Christmas is supposed to be a family time, but for me it is a time when I feel torn in two. I wish I could spend half the day with Mum and half the day with Dad and then that would be fair. Instead I spend alternate Christmases and New Years with each of my parents and it's really, really hard.' The pain is relived every year for teenagers when there is such a background of sadness. All we can do is recognize that there are many more painful conversations like this than there used to be and try to help people in those situations to have hope as well as anguish.

Painful conversations that help us move on

It is often painful to ask for forgiveness when a relationship has turned sour or some external factor has thrown it off course. But the pain of asking for forgiveness is sometimes at the centre of relationships that grow. I am on a governing body with Jimmy Dunn, a distinguished Emeritus Professor of New Testament at the University of Durham. As a biblical scholar he is utterly rigorous. As a committee member he is equally focused. We talked about good conversations. He said that forgiveness is at the heart of conversations, and that conversations are the dynamic of community. Saying 'thank you' is at the heart of conversations that bind, but saying 'sorry' is also an essential part of conversation. We all make mistakes of one sort or another. For Jimmy conversations that bind the community together include, in particular, those in which we say we are learning by our mistakes and we seek each other's forgiveness. When we say 'sorry' and receive the forgiveness of another person, that brings a whole new dimension to the joy of conversation. For some conversations to be successful there has to be a painful beginning in which forgiveness is shared.

Conversations with friends are the substance of life. If you analyse these conversations, they are often full of news and reflections. When the two friends feel mutually safe, these conversations involve deep sharing, searching and sometimes confession. We are missing a whole dimension of the depth of friendship if our conversations with friends do not take us into painful territory. Sometimes hiding away pain makes it more destructive. Sharing painful memories in conversation can sometimes put them in a new perspective and enable us to move on. Although the conversation is, in one sense, painful because it is bringing out the pain, its therapeutic quality is of huge value.

Lessons from doctors

A doctor's life is full of painful conversations. One consultant told me that when telling somebody that they were going to die he would talk with them about the dignity of dying gracefully and the importance of completing conversations over the remaining months with all those dear to them. Another consultant told me that so many of his colleagues gave painful news abruptly and badly. His approach was to share bad news carefully and thoughtfully and never in a rush.

A GP shared with me the importance of giving bad news in the context of a relationship of trust between doctor and patient. Her aim was to build up the type of relationship with her patients that was able to cope with the bad news: it was important to build up such a credit of goodwill and understanding with each patient that painful news could be absorbed within that relationship. This approach is relevant for relationships well beyond medicine. Strong relationships need to grow in such a way that they can absorb the possibility of painful conversations at some stage.

Another GP told me of the importance of never leaving someone isolated when you have given them painful news. The support arrangements need to be clear. She also said that when passing on painful news she never wanted people to give up hope. She would always be frank about the nature of the bad news when there was a pessimistic prognosis, but her approach was to encourage the patient to remain hopeful. The aim was not to be unrealistic but to encourage each patient to be positive. If a patient came out of a painful conversation viewing the future positively, there was a much greater chance – though obviously no promise – of remission.

Within a busy day a doctor must switch from patient to patient. This means a joyful conversation one minute with a recovering patient and a painful conversation the next with a patient who is facing death. This is a remarkable test of a doctor's communication skills, as he or she strives to address successfully the needs of such very different people. The rest of us are seldom involved in quite such a rapid oscillation between joyful and painful conversations. We can, however, learn so much from the approach that doctors take, particularly how to build up that bank of goodwill which enables painful conversations to take place within a context of trust.

Coping with pain

External appearances do not always show the whole truth. Sometimes when we have an opportunity to have a long conversation with somebody they reveal the pain behind cheery eyes. I had a long conversation recently with a lady who was a former colleague. She is always cheerful and bright. I knew her as an encourager.

She told me that exactly a year earlier she had had a painful conversation with her husband. He announced that he did not love her any more and was moving out. She was shocked and hurt. He returned four months later. They are now rubbing along in an OK sort of way. She loves him dearly, but now recognizes that the depth of love may not be equal. Sometimes she wants to talk with him about their relationship and where it is going, but he brushes these requests aside and does not want to talk.

She is in her mid–40s. The opportunity for children has come and gone. Life is sometimes painful. She struggles to get up in the morning and brave the day. When she is at work life is good. She is an appreciator and is admired by those around her. But sometimes she feels 'rubbish'. She thinks she has not used her brain. She worries that she is not being useful in life. She does not necessarily believe me when I say she is a wonderful encourager and a positive influence on those around her.

The painful conversation she had when her husband said he wanted to leave still hurts. She wants to have more conversations with her husband now that he is back. She recognizes that they may be painful too, but it is even more painful that her husband does not want to talk. She hides this pain very effectively from the people she knows. There is perhaps not much her friends can do to help other than be there, keep encouraging her and be a positive presence to help her live with the pain. No one can solve it for her. She recognizes that she needs and wants to live positively with the decision she has made. That does not reduce the pain, but it puts it into context. She is a brave lady.

People often put a very brave face on what would otherwise be a painful conversation. Matthew Pinsent tells the story (in *The Times*, 4 December 2004) of when Alex Partridge had to withdraw from the crew which eventually won a rowing gold medal at the Athens Olympics. Alex had suffered a stress fracture. The specialist said to him, 'This is really dangerous. I'm afraid I've got bad news.' Alex actually had a punctured lung. He could not train and he could not go to the Olympics. Matthew said that his inclination would have been to shake the hands of the other members of the crew, say goodbye and disappear. But Alex did not go anywhere. He stayed with the crew and bombarded them with text messages full of advice, encouragement and banter.

As Alex watched the television reports of the rowing from London he shared in all their joy. He said that sometimes he thought, 'Thank God it's not me,' but he wanted to be inside the boat too. Alex talked of the races with a smile on his face. Matthew said that he had expected to tread on eggshells around Alex since the victory in Athens, but not a bit of it. Alex got excited, joined in the celebrations and has thrown himself into a new four-year campaign. This is a wonderful story of coping with a painful situation, not by running away from it but by being a positive, cheerful influence within it. Alex could not compete in the final, but no one could have been more supportive to his colleagues than he was.

Sometimes the prospect of a painful conversation is worse than the reality. A friend was working in a voluntary organization with young people. After a few unguarded comments, a parent of one of the young people sent a strongly worded letter to my friend and his boss. My friend found this disturbing. He thought he ought to talk to the parent, but found it difficult to raise the courage to do so. After encouragement he did have a long conversation with that parent. This difficult relationship had preyed on his mind over recent weeks, but to his immense relief the two of them had an excellent conversation with a very positive resolution. During the discussion they were both nearly in tears and the conversation turned out to be both important and healing. The initial incident had produced emotional reactions which caused attitudes to get out of proportion.

What made this painful conversation work?

- They created space for a reflective conversation to take place.
- There was a willingness and keenness on behalf of both parties to talk the problem through and find a resolution.
- There was a sense of confession as both acknowledged that they had over-reacted.
- There was an awareness and a sharing of the emotional context and feelings: the parent was able to share the background from her previous experiences which had led to the critical reaction.
- There was a keenness to sort out the issue and move on.
- There was agreement about the next steps, which would include a stock-take discussion two months later.

For my friend a load had been lifted off his mind. He knew that he was partly at fault and could not understand why the whole episode had got out of proportion in his mind. He was immensely relieved and joyful that he and the parent could move on in their relationship. He was so glad that he had found the courage to raise this issue. He had expected a painful conversation, but in reality it was such a relief to be at one with this parent that it turned into an almost joyful conversation.

Some of our most painful conversations are inevitably around bereavement. Some of the saddest conversations I have ever had were when I was telling people that my mother had died. I was conscious in many of these conversations that they were even more painful to other people than they were to me. Telling an 85-year-old that their friend of 50 years' standing had died felt almost as if I was putting another nail into that elderly person's coffin. Sometimes it is not that easy to find a gentle way of giving painful news, but if it can be done face to face by a relative or close friend it can make such a difference.

Preparing for painful conversations

A youth worker at a church shared with me the range of painful conversations that he had with young people. He was also anxious to point out, however, that many of his conversations were joyful ones, as both young people and parents would offer very fulsome thanks for the work my friend was doing. Sometimes there would be very painful conversations with young people as they shared some of their personal hurt, for example the death of a grandma or lack of success in exams. Sometimes the conversations would move rapidly between different subjects and the hurt would only come out after trust had been established and other subjects had been discussed. My friend's role was crucial in enabling these young people to talk through painful and personal issues. What caused him most pain was the occasional criticism from parents when he had simply tried to be open and constructive with the young people.

Painful conversations occur as much at work as at home. In some ways it is easier at work, as you are only there for part of the day. Painful conversations at work occur when there are marked differences of view and when difficult decisions need to be taken. There is no easy way to tell somebody that they have been made redundant. There is no easy way to tell somebody that their performance is not up to scratch. But out of painful conversations so often comes good. How can this be?

- For someone made redundant, their situation may lead to new horizons and new opportunities. The transition may take them to places where they had never envisaged going before.
- When there are hard messages about performance, it may mean that somebody addresses those issues in a way that they have never done before, gaining a new confidence that takes them on into new possibilities.

All these painful conversations require the same sort of preparation.

- Prepare the facts carefully.
- Create the right space – private, quiet and not too rushed – for the conversation.
- Give the news simply and clearly.
- Understand how somebody is likely to react and be sensitive to that in the way you put the news across.
- Demonstrate care and compassion in the way you relay the news.
- Give the person time to reflect on the bad news.
- Be there to absorb the initial reaction.
- Try to be as supportive as possible in taking forward the next steps.

We do sometimes carry with us for ever the memories of painful conversations. Perhaps we had some difficult conversations with our parents. Those memories have been parked in our minds for a long while. Maybe the pictures of those conversations have become bigger and bigger. They have become dragons that need to be slain.

Maybe we have regrets that when someone died we had never had a conversation of reconciliation with them. It is sometimes worth taking stock of memories of painful conversations and seeing whether there is some way to achieve a reconciliation which will turn that painful memory into something much more positive.

We can sometimes inadvertently turn a conversation into a painful experience by the way we end it. The sudden discontinuation of a conversation can be deeply offensive. It is possible to be 'dropped' without warning from a conversation at a social event when someone else 'more interesting' comes into the room: the person with whom you are conversing suddenly becomes distant or vague or even starts blatantly looking over your shoulder at some activity or person in the distance. This can cause a surprising amount of pain.

The ending of conversations is just as important as the beginning. The more encouraging a conversation, the more painful it can become if the ending is wrong. Moving on gracefully from one conversation to another is so important. This is helped by strong eye contact at the end of a conversation and by the tone of voice in the concluding sentences. Some reference to a future discussion or 'looking forward to meeting you again' leaves a conversation ending in a generous and open way. We forget the way we end conversations at our peril – and this is true for all types of conversations, not just painful ones.

It is just too painful to talk about some things. My father-in-law had been a doctor with the British forces and landed in Normandy two days after D-Day. On one occasion he said very briefly that he had been close to death on three occasions and never wanted to talk about it. We never pressed him. Those memories were too painful to share. Maybe it would have been good if he had talked about it, but we knew that we must respect absolutely his wish not to enter that territory. Within close relationships there are inevitably going to be some territories that are too painful to enter in conversation. That situation must be respected.

Next steps

Against the background that painful conversations come in many different shapes and sizes, the principles from the start of the chapter continue to be relevant.

- **Start with understanding**. Always try to put yourself in the shoes of the other person. What are they thinking and feeling? How will this particular news or conversation affect them? What is likely to be their reaction and how can you best prepare for that? It is so important not to pretend that your understanding is greater than it is. There is nothing so irritating to a person who has become severely disabled to be told, 'I know how you feel,' when the visitor cannot possibly know how that person feels. 'Understanding' is counterproductive if overdone.
- **Be focused**. This is about effective preparation and articulating clearly the message you are conveying. It is sometimes about not being diverted by your own or the other person's emotional reaction. Jesus' focus in conversation never seemed to diminish: it was a crucial part of his persona.
- **Be consistent**. Building on the trust you have with the person to whom you are talking is crucial. Consistency

in the way you talk and express views is essential to ensuring that trust is maintained strongly through the conversation.

- **Be sensitive to your own emotions**. Be prepared to be surprised by your own reactions. Sometimes the reactions will be about your own pain, sometimes you will have difficulty speaking, and at other times you will want to remove yourself from the situation as rapidly as possible. The more self-aware we are about our own emotional reactions, the more effectively we can prepare for that and not let our reactions detract from the conversation. Sometimes our reactions will be an essential part of the dynamic in the conversation. At other times they can distort our perspective. The difficulty lies in trying to be sensitive to whether our own reaction is being helpful or unhelpful.

- **Share pain**. This is about being present and allowing yourself to echo the pain and reflect back your responses to the other person's feelings. In this quiet, reflective way you can absorb some of that pain.

- **Leave space**. This is partially about privacy, but also about leaving silence so that there is opportunity for reflection and moving on. Never feel that you have to rush into any silence or fill it with words.

- **Move on**. Whenever any painful conversation ends there needs to be some clarity, explicit or implicit, about next steps. This may involve reflecting further, or possibly making an agreement to have a subsequent conversation. This final phase of moving on should not be ignored. Drawing conclusions is an important part of letting both people move on.

- **Offer continuing support**. Helping to build someone up is about offering support at painful times. It is also about your continuing availability. Just the offer of ongoing help, even if it is not taken up, can be such an encouragement.

These principles relate particularly to initiating a painful conversation. Sometimes we will be the person in pain in that conversation, and in that case the same themes apply. Perhaps the most important aspect is that we are open to our pain and ready to move on, to be supported and sometimes challenged.

Questions for reflection

1. How painful do you think Jesus found the conversations with the rich young ruler and with the disciples at Gethsemane?
2. What lessons do you draw from the way Jesus handled these painful conversations?
3. What examples stand out for you of particularly painful conversations that you have been part of, both as giver and receiver of painful news?
4. How do you think you can best prepare when you need to give bad news in painful conversations?
5. How do you respond if someone else initiates a painful conversation with you? Are there ways in which you would like to respond differently?
6. How can you prepare yourself better to cope with painful conversations?
7. When you are in pain, how can conversation best help you to move on through that pain?

Unresponsive conversations

7

Our days are full of unresponsive conversations. Maybe they are not conversations at all! There are attempts at conversations that don't work. At other times the conversations are unresponsive because somebody is pre-occupied. Sometimes it is because the walls are up and there is no willingness at that point to engage emotionally. How do we cope with unresponsive conversations? Sometimes we persist when perhaps we should not. At other times we withdraw gracefully and wait for a better opportunity. We have to accept the reality that some conversations will always be unresponsive. Sometimes we are unresponsive ourselves and cause pain to others without realizing it. Unresponsive conversations take many different forms and are often very painful.

Our two examples from the life of Jesus are the unresponsive conversations he had with Judas at Gethsemane and with God on the cross.

> While he was still speaking a crowd came up, and the man who was called Judas, one of the Twelve, was leading them. He approached Jesus to kiss him, but Jesus asked him, 'Judas, are you betraying the Son of Man with a kiss?'
>
> When Jesus' followers saw what was going to

happen, they said, 'Lord, should we strike with our swords?' And one of them struck the servant of the high priest, cutting off his right ear.

But Jesus answered, 'No more of this!' And he touched the man's ear and healed him.

Then Jesus said to the chief priests, the officers of the temple guard, and the elders, who had come for him, 'Am I leading a rebellion, that you have come with swords and clubs? Every day I was with you in the temple courts, and you did not lay a hand on me. But this is your hour – when darkness reigns.' (Lk. 22.47–53)

When Judas approached Jesus to kiss him Jesus asked, 'Judas, are you betraying the Son of Man with a kiss?' There is no evidence that Judas responded to that question. Jesus was remarkably restrained. When one of his disciples struck a servant of the high priest and cut off his right ear, Jesus insisted, 'No more of this!' and healed the injured man. Even when he was being taken captive, he was compassionate about the welfare of the high priest's servant. Jesus spoke levelly to the temple guard: 'Am I leading a rebellion, that you have come with swords and clubs? . . . This is your hour – when darkness reigns.' He was not provoked into anger: he remained compassionate and clear in all he said.

The second passage comes just prior to Jesus' death on the cross.

At the sixth hour darkness came over the whole land until the ninth hour. And at the ninth hour Jesus cried out in a loud voice, '*Eloi, Eloi, lama sabachthani?*' – which means, 'My God, my God, why have you forsaken me?'

When some of those standing near heard this, they said, 'Listen, he's calling Elijah.'

One man ran, filled a sponge with wine vinegar, put it on a stick, and offered it to Jesus to drink. 'Now leave him alone. Let's see if Elijah comes to take him down,' he said.

With a loud cry, Jesus breathed his last.

The curtain of the temple was torn in two from top to bottom. And when the centurion, who stood there in front of Jesus, heard his cry and saw how he died, he said, 'Surely this man was the Son of God!' (Mk 15.33–39)

Jesus is showing the depth of his humanity. In great pain on the cross, with nails through his hands and feet, Jesus cried out in a loud voice, 'My God, my God, why have you forsaken me?' And then, with a loud cry, he breathed his last.

Jesus was caught in what must have felt like inescapable darkness. It was as if God had left him alone to die in extreme bleakness. The reality was that Jesus would be resurrected from the dead, but at this point all seemed lost and Jesus was talking in the blackness of an apparently unresponsive conversation.

What are the key themes that come out of these conversations?

- **Be clear**. In both stories Jesus was very straightforward in what he said. To Judas he said, 'Are you betraying the Son of Man with a kiss?' and to God he said, 'Why have you forsaken me?' Even though they were unresponsive, Jesus was absolutely clear and straightforward in starting those conversations. He was not put off by the potential for unresponsiveness.

- **Don't always assume there is an answer**. On neither occasion did Jesus assume that his comments would lead to a two-way conversation. He made the first step, but had to accept the fact that no dialogue followed.
- **Don't be provoked**. Jesus held back the disciples, who wanted to fight the temple guard. He accepted the silence on the cross as he died.
- **Be compassionate**. Jesus was about to be taken away for trial. His instinctive response was to bring healing to the injured servant rather than to look after himself first.
- **Sometimes darkness is unavoidable**. Not every conversation has a positive response. There was an atmosphere of bleakness as Jesus was taken away to be tried. There was a sense of emptiness as he died on the cross.
- **Be ready to move on**. Jesus accepted that he had to leave Gethsemane and go to face trial. He accepted his death on the cross. Both were steps that eventually led to the resurrection.
- **Healing takes time**. In neither story did Jesus assume that healing was instantaneous. All would be well in time, but there were other steps to take and other pains to bear first.

Unresponsive conversations take many forms. We will look at the most significant of these over the course of this chapter.

Children who cannot yet speak

Although the newly born child may show no immediate response other than crying, that in no way reduces the warmth and affection felt between parent and child. Parents begin to look for any flicker of response and will celebrate each new development. The absence of a verbal response does not lessen the strength of the relationship. Fairly quickly babies follow their mothers' faces and respond with their eyes and bodies to their parents' actions. The conversation may not be in words, but it is rich in emotions and the joys of intimacy.

Teenagers who are determined to be unresponsive

In the UK in the 1990s there was a fictional TV programme involving two teenagers, Kevin and Perry. They only responded in grunts to their parents, even though they could be perfectly civilized to other adults. In the wake of the programme, to be named 'Kevin' was a synonym for unresponsive, boorish behaviour. Often a good way to get unresponsive, teenagers to laugh and to talk about how they feel is to invite them to watch a few episodes about Kevin and Perry!

A youth worker friend told me of the range of unresponsive conversations he has with young people. Initially they will simply observe and give one-word answers. Then they will begin to talk about the subjects they are interested in – football, music, sometimes even school work. Often they will want to jump around between one subject and another in order to test out whether the youth worker is really interested in them or not. The youth worker has to pass a test of his willingness to engage on a wide range of issues before the teenager will want to talk about anything that is in any way personal. The scattergun approach to conversation is often a smokescreen and a necessary process that has to be gone through first. Once common interests and trust are established, the youngster may well want to open up and be responsive about issues of real importance.

Many teenagers suffer from a huge pressure of expect-ation from their parents. In an age when achievement is regarded as so important, it is perhaps inevitable that many parents will want to push their children towards attaining the best possible examination results and delivering achievements in many different spheres. It is not surprising that, faced with this weight of expectation, youngsters can become aloof or detached. Parents then become exces-sively worried when their youngsters are not as responsive as they think they should be. Often the teenagers only want to talk at the most inconvenient moments, such as at 11 o'clock at night when their parents are desperate to go to bed. By contrast, it is sad to say that in some cases parents are not interested enough in the lives of their teenagers to bother putting any pressure on them at all, and this lack of interest is even more damaging than too much interest.

Working constructively through unresponsive con-versations with teenagers is all about observing the fol-lowing principles.

- Being secure in a long-term relationship which can cope with different phases.
- Demonstrating a continuity of love whatever the absence of words.

- Keeping a focus on the areas of common interest and sharing (shared meals, films and music).
- Being patient, and patient again.
- Being positive in the belief that the seeds which were sown in the early years will come to fruition in due course.
- Accepting that young people are not made in our own image, and have their own identity and lives, and should be allowed to make their own decisions.

Coping with unresponsive conversations with teenagers is about loving them anyway, accepting that we are all different and enabling them to make their own way.

Older people with dementia

In her early 80s my mother suffered a minor stroke, but she was determined to keep control of her life. She was fiercely independent and dreaded the day when her memory would begin to go. As the strokes became more frequent, her memory did begin to slip away and we recognized the first signs of dementia. She could not live alone and needed constant care. Her memory for names and dates began to disappear. She became less responsive.

Right to the end, however, she did respond to a smile, to someone holding her hand and to words from the Psalms that she knew well. My youngest son (then aged 13) would read to her some of the best known psalms: her face would light up and she would echo some of the phrases.

In her last months we tried to take account of her lack of ability to respond. Her room was full of photographs.

We showed her pictures from different phases of her life, many of which brought back a smile. Her childhood was more real to her than recent years. There was very little response about recent events, but much more about events long ago. Memories of the Sunday school outings she went on as a child remained as vivid as ever. It was important that we worked with the grain of her memory, so that we were as responsive to her as we possibly could be within the limitations of her health.

Hugh Montefiore, Bishop of Birmingham in the 1980s, writes very sensitively about the effects of Alzheimer's disease on his wife and the changing nature of their conversations. Hugh was an energetic and controversial leader and a man of great compassion. Brought up in a Jewish family, he converted to Christianity. In his auto-biography *Oh God, What Next* he says that his affection for his parents was undiminished, as was theirs for him, but there was inevitably a certain restraint between them. His wife, Elizabeth, was an Anglican. They waited until after the Second World War to get married. Hugh Montefiore wrote, 'I did not expect to come back from the War, and I did not want to leave Elizabeth a widow, still less leave behind a single-parent family. Nor, until Hitler was beaten, did I want her to marry a Jew, for her own safety's sake. Better wait and if I did come back, we would be married.'

During his later days in Birmingham Elizabeth gradually became ill. Soon after Hugh retired, the verdict from the hospital was that she had Alzheimer's. He writes,

All through the overloaded diaries of the last 20 or 30 years I have told myself and told her: 'At least we can be together when I retire.' Yes, that was true, but what sort of being together was it going to be? Meanwhile, what? We decided there was no point in trying to paint the town red while we could. Holidays, yes; but let us enjoy as much as we could the many blessings of ordinary life which we usually take for granted.

. . . She cared for me so wonderfully and so loyally through all the difficulties of my ministry. Elizabeth always accepted me, and she had provided a calmness and serenity which my impetuous nature craved.

. . . The really terrible time was when she was finding things difficult, and realised what was to come. The best thing was just to hug her tight and to go on hugging her until the moment passed. She preferred not to discuss the future with me, so we didn't.

. . . Sometimes I think back to what Elizabeth was, and I have been reduced to tears when I have left her for respite care in the hospital ward with the human wrecks who are its permanent inhabitants. But then I recollect myself and realise this is only self-pity. I can no longer feel really bad about how she feels. Now that she no longer has any idea what is happening, and certainly can't remember anything at all of what she once was, she is really quite happy for most of the time, once one gets the medication right. She cannot speak much now, although occasionally there are flashes of the old Eliza, and she can still use those admirable 'cover up' words which she employed to hide her inability to answer questions – 'perhaps' or 'possibly' or 'probably'. She no longer knows my name but she can smile, and occasionally she says 'I love you'; or more probably she gets her pronouns confused and says 'She likes him'.

In cases of dementia, it is worth remembering these crucial points for conversations.

- Share some conversation on issues or topics where conversation is still possible. Keep the focus on those areas.
- Create the space for togetherness that may well include very few words.
- Spend time on conversations with others outside this painful world, so that the conversation with the individual suffering from dementia can be entered and exited in a way that leaves the rest of your world in a reasonable state of stability.

The wrong timing

I am told that when I return home from London each evening, for the first few minutes I do not listen. My family say that I need to have a shower and a glass of water before I am worth talking to. I am not as conscious of this behaviour as they are, but apparently it happens every day. Frances knows that the most productive time to enter conversation is when I have 'come to'.

Teenagers, in particular, are very sensitive about the timing being right. In our experience the best conversations come not at the time of our choosing, but at the time of their choosing. Adaptability in responding to the timing of their needs is central to effective conversations with them.

Often you do not know that the timing is wrong until you begin the conversation. A fast diplomatic withdrawal is then the right course of action. But we often do develop a sensitivity to the right moment for different types of conversation. Perhaps the main thing is to keep asking the question, 'Is the timing right?' and then not to be too put out if the answer to that question is 'Not now.'

Friendships that die

Some friendships and the conversations that go with them continue for ever. Other friendships reach their natural conclusion and end up as an annual exchange of Christmas cards. Inevitably, when we go through the Christmas card list, we will feel sad that with some people there is virtually no contact. In some cases it is right to renew that friendship, but on other occasions attempts to do so produce an unresponsive reaction and it is clearly time to move on.

Feeling alone: locked inside

There are moments when you want to be by yourself. You do not want to respond to cheery comments from others. You are locked inside. Sometimes, if you are suffering from depression, it is very comforting to be locked inside. On other occasions we need to be taken out of ourselves and forced to be responsive.

The best of friends will know when to leave us alone and when to put us on the spot to stretch us into being more responsive. When we are feeling alone and unresponsive, one way forward is to put ourselves into different situations with different people to see what our level of responsiveness is like. When we find some people who do enable us to come out of ourselves, they are probably the ones people to be with over the next phase.

No willingness to listen

We all think of ourselves as reasonable people prepared to listen to the concerns and arguments of others. Often, however, we are actually very blinkered. We may well block out what people are saying to us – even if only subconsciously – as a means of self-protection.

A key question is, 'Am I deluding myself?' If we are putting on very firm blinkers and not changing when we should, then the honest views of people we trust should be the most important influence upon us. We may well be unresponsive and not know that this is the case. Hence the value of asking our friends and colleagues whether they think we are listening and responding effectively.

I can remember a number of people with whom I worked who never seemed to listen to what was said about their performance or contribution. Constructive criticism seemed to flow like water off a duck's back. They were given repeated opportunities but never seemed to respond. They heard the words but never acted on them. The unresponsiveness in the conversation occurred because they were somehow blinded to the reality of their own personal impact upon others. Sometimes this was a result of their cultural background and at other times it was a consequence of the way they protected themselves.

When you are in regular conversation with someone who appears to listen but never responds, the key to coping with that frustration is to try to understand the reasons why that person is so unresponsive. It may well mean talking through very gently with them your perception about their lack of responsiveness and asking them to share openly what is going on in their mind and their heart. Then you may be able to journey together towards a resolution.

Limited response

I can remember a sequence of encouraging conversations with one person. He said he was determined to do things differently, but the change never really happened. I believed very firmly that he could change, but when he did not and there were major problems I was held partially responsible. In management terms I should have been tougher. In personal terms I believed the individual's commitment to change. I believed that the responsiveness he showed in our conversations was a positive attempt to move on. Perhaps I believed in this person too much.

If you have been in a leadership role at work or church or in a voluntary organization, you are likely to have experienced this situation: you receive a clear initial responsiveness from someone, but there follows only limited change. In these cases we are faced with a dilemma. How much generosity of spirit should we show as somebody tries to improve, and when is it right to be hard-nosed for the benefit of the whole organization?

Inability to respond

In an article in *The Times* (4 December 2004) Helen Rumbelo tells the tragic story of some prostitutes in London. She travels with two Vice Squad officers who identify Catrina on a street corner. Catrina greets the sergeant like an old friend – he arrested her last month – and begins a good-natured negotiation. 'Go away!' laughs Catrina. 'No, you go away,' says the sergeant, smiling back. She pleads to be left alone for three hours so that she can earn some money. 'But if you do that we'll arrest you.'

Her response is, 'You know I don't care, it's half an hour in the warm to me.' She walks away, but 15 minutes later she is standing on the same corner and is arrested for loitering. As soon as she gets into the car her chirpy attitude dissolves into sobs. 'It just seems like there's nothing I can do to change my life,' she says. She has been addicted to heroin and crack for three years and it will take her one or two extra 'tricks' to work off a £40 fine from the magistrates, before she can earn any money for drugs. She pleads, 'The only thing which would get me off the street is drug rehab, but there never seem to be any places.' What a sad set of circumstances, and a sad set of unresponsive conversations between Catrina and the police, in which Catrina is caught in a web that is so difficult to escape.

Moving on from unresponsive conversations

When someone does not respond, do you persist or bow out? The individual going through grief may initially not want to respond at all. The good friend is patient and puts out gentle feelers. One day the individual may be ready to respond. The good parent keeps talking to the teenager, and hopefully one day they will respond in a cheerful, responsive way.

Sometimes there is no response. When do you persist and when do you give up? Sometimes there comes a point when you say 'enough is enough'. The good priest will want to respond to all parishioners, but when the relationship with some is unresponsive it is unfair on the other people to persist with it. There are occasions when it is right to recognize that limited time and energy demand that we focus on people who can and do respond. There is a difficult balance here. Sometimes it is right to persist; on other occasions it is right to draw a line and move on. Judging which way to go is never straightforward. We can want to 'shake the dust off our feet' too rapidly. Peace of mind requires that we push the door more than once. When close family members are involved we will never want to give up, but with members of our community or work colleagues there will be a moment when it must be right to move on.

Respecting areas of privacy

There are some conversations which it is best not to have. For each of us there are aspects of our lives that are very private. We do not particularly want other people to enter those areas. We do not invite them in and we would not thank them for inviting themselves in. Those private areas are a matter between ourselves and our Maker. It is right to be open about every aspect of our life in prayer, but sometimes it is also perfectly right for certain areas of our lives to be off limits to others with no response invited or given. If this is true for us, it will be true for other people too. There are moments when recognizing the boundaries is absolutely crucial. We push too hard at our peril. Some areas are best left unresponsive, and we need to try to develop a sensitivity for those areas.

Next steps

Having looked at different types of unresponsive conversations, we return now to our opening themes. What practical guidelines can we draw from them?

- **Be clear**. Always be clear about your starting point and the issues that are important to you. Then be selective about what you say and how you say it.
- **Don't always assume there is an answer**. Don't be put off or downhearted if there is no response. The timing may not be right. Jesus got no immediate answer to his question from the cross. The words we say may still be being considered, even though there is no obvious response. Sometimes more time is needed for reflection or healing.
- **Don't be provoked**. If you are confident in what you want to say and why you want to say it, and if you have thought through your reactions to different situations, there is no need to be provoked. The more you have imagined yourself in somebody else's shoes, the less likely you are to be taken aback by their reaction and provoked. An emotional reaction as a result of being provoked rarely helps. So take a deep breath and stand back. Jesus was a model of restraint when Judas betrayed him.
- **Be compassionate**. Never let your heart be hardened. Keep that generosity of spirit. Even when someone's pain is self-inflicted, try to keep the compassion that upholds your love for that person. Particular compassion is needed when people – for whatever reason – cannot respond.
- **Sometimes darkness is unavoidable**. Sometimes there will be no response. It will seem bleak. Accept

that this is an experience shared by everyone. It was certainly Jesus' experience on the cross. Try to be able to say, 'So be it.' Try not to take it as a personal criticism.

- **Be ready to move on**. Accept that in any unresponsive conversation there is a time to move on into other spheres of your life. One unresponsive conversation is not the end of the world, even though it may be very painful.

- **Healing takes time**. The pain caused by unresponsive conversations does not go away easily. Friendships can be damaged so readily when trust is broken. Healing does happen, but it needs to be worked at. It is not easy to accept that sometimes after an unresponsive conversation a friendship needs to be left for a period. Only after a passage of time can healing really begin.

Questions for reflection

1. How would you have reacted to Judas if he had betrayed you?
2. God was responsive to Jesus in the long run but not the short run. Is that sometimes your experience too?
3. What sort of unresponsive conversations have caused you most grief?
4. How do you personally best handle unresponsive conversations?
5. What particular situations do you face now in which there are unresponsive conversations? Are these within your family, your community or your workplace?
6. Are there examples of unresponsive conversations you have had where it has been right to give up?

7. What keeps you going in unresponsive conversations?
8. How might the principles gathered in this chapter help?

Joyful conversations

8

Have you been surprised by the joy in some conversations? Often the joy is unexpected. You are in the midst of a painful or challenging conversation. All of a sudden there is a flash of humour: laughter defuses a tense situation and the conversation moves on into a different phase. Touches of joy uplift any conversation. Joyful conversations are essential for our well-being. Enjoying joyful conversations is not self-indulgence; it is an essential part of sharing in each other's humanity. It is about warmth, pleasure, connecting with people and sharing good memories and humour.

The Oxford English Dictionary defines joy as 'pleasurable emotion due to well-being or satisfaction; the feeling or state of being highly pleased; exultation of spirit; gladness, delight'. Joy is one of the most intense of emotions. Shakespeare describes King Richard II as weeping for joy 'to stand upon my kingdom once again'. Samuel Taylor Coleridge in 'The Rime of the Ancient Mariner' talks of the travellers' 'silent joy' when they arrive at their appointed rest and their native country. The psalmists talk of the fullness of joy in God's presence. For Mother Teresa, 'a joyful heart is the normal result of a heart burning with love'. Shared joy is part of the rich tapestry of conversations. We can gain so much if we encourage the joyful dimension of conversations, be it within the family, the community or the workplace.

After Jesus has washed the feet of the disciples there is a conversation between Jesus and Peter which contains a remarkable outburst of joy from Peter.

It was just before the Passover Feast. Jesus knew that the time had come for him to leave this world and go to the Father. Having loved his own who were in the world, he now showed them the full extent of his love.

The evening meal was being served, and the devil had already prompted Judas Iscariot, son of Simon, to betray Jesus. Jesus knew that the Father had put all things under his power, and that he had come from God and was returning to God; so he got up from the meal, took off his outer clothing, and wrapped a towel round his waist. After that, he poured water into a basin and began to wash his disciples' feet, drying them with the towel that was wrapped round him.

He came to Simon Peter, who said to him, 'Lord, are you going to wash my feet?'

Jesus replied, 'You do not realise now what I am doing, but later you will understand.'

'No,' said Peter, 'you shall never wash my feet.'

Jesus answered, 'Unless I wash you, you have no part with me.'

'Then, Lord,' Simon Peter replied, 'not just my feet but my hands and my head as well!'

Jesus answered, 'A person who has had a bath needs only to wash his feet; his whole body is clean. And you are clean, though not every one of you.' For he knew who was going to betray him, and that was why he said not every one was clean.

When he had finished washing their feet, he put on his clothes and returned to his place. 'Do you understand what I have done for you?' he asked them. 'You call me "Teacher" and "Lord", and rightly so, for that is what I am. Now that I, your Lord and Teacher, have washed your feet, you also should wash one another's feet. I have set you an example that you should do as I have done for you. I tell you the truth, no servant is greater than his master, nor is a messenger greater than the one who sent him. Now that you know these things, you will be blessed if you do them.' (Jn 13.1–17)

At this meal Jesus takes his colleagues by surprise as he removes his outer clothing and wraps a towel round his waist. He then pours water into a basin and washes the disciples' feet. Then comes the wonderful exchange with Peter. Initially there is a sense of surprise from Peter that Jesus is going to wash his feet. He asserts, 'No, you shall never wash my feet.' Jesus is insistent: 'Unless I wash you, you have no part with me.' Then we read the joyful response from Peter, 'Not just my feet but my hands and my head as well!' Peter is pouring out his love for Jesus. These are words of dedication, full of joyful commitment. Perhaps they are expressed so dramatically because of the emotional sensitivity of the moment.

Jesus goes on to draw out of this scene a practical lesson about no servant being greater than his master. The message comes over all the more strongly because of the dramatic and joyful exchange with Peter. Jesus uses the physical act of washing feet as a powerful symbol that leads into this joyful interchange. This is an impressive illustration of how a symbolic act can add to the impact of a joyful conversation.

Our second example comes from the joyful conversations after the resurrection between Jesus and Mary Magdalene and then with the disciples.

Then the disciples went back to their homes, but Mary stood outside the tomb crying. As she wept, she bent over to look into the tomb and saw two angels in white, seated where Jesus' body had been, one at the head and the other at the foot.

They asked her, 'Woman, why are you crying?'

'They have taken my Lord away,' she said, 'and I don't know where they have put him.' At this, she turned round and saw Jesus standing there, but she did not realise that it was Jesus.

'Woman,' he said, 'why are you crying? Who is it you are looking for?'

Thinking he was the gardener, she said, 'Sir, if you have carried him away, tell me where you have put him, and I will get him.'

Jesus said to her, 'Mary.'

She turned towards him and cried out in Aramaic, 'Rabboni!' (which means Teacher).

Jesus said, 'Do not hold on to me, for I have not yet returned to the Father. Go instead to my brothers and tell them, "I am returning to my Father and your Father, to my God and your God."'

Mary Magdalene went to the disciples with the news: 'I have seen the Lord!' And she told them that he had said these things to her.

On the evening of that first day of the week, when the disciples were together, with the doors locked for fear of the Jews, Jesus came and stood among them and said, 'Peace be with you!' After he said this, he showed them his hands and side. The disciples were overjoyed when they saw the Lord.

Again Jesus said, 'Peace be with you! As the Father has sent me, I am sending you.' And with that he breathed on them and said, 'Receive the Holy Spirit. If you forgive anyone his sins, they are forgiven; if you do not forgive them, they are not forgiven.' (Jn 20.10–23)

The disciples and close followers of Jesus were heart-broken after his crucifixion. Mary Magdalene is in tears outside the tomb. She talks to a man in the garden whom she does not recognize. She pleads with the man to tell her where the body of Jesus now lies. The man utters just one word, 'Mary', and she cries out with joy, 'Rabboni!' There are no wasted words, but this is an intense moment of communication. Jesus is quietly present with Mary Magdalene. He asks a gentle question of Mary first: 'Why are you crying? Who is it you are looking for?' Jesus gives Mary some space first, before showing who he is.

Later on, the resurrected Jesus meets the disciples. He stands among them and says the brief words, 'Peace be with you!' The disciples are overjoyed. The conversation does not stop there, however. Jesus allows the disciples to be immersed in this moment of joy, and then he moves straight into the announcement, 'I am sending you.' He turns their joy from an inward to an outward perspective by breathing on them and commissioning them as they receive the Holy Spirit.

There are other examples of joyful conversations between Jesus and his disciples: for example when the disciples come back from early missions all excited and Jesus is evidently joyful at their reports (Lk. 10.17–22).

From the joyful conversations Jesus had we can identify the following themes.

- **The importance of surprise**. Peter was not expecting Jesus to wash the disciples' feet. It was the surprise of this act which helped create the context for the joyful conversation between Peter and Jesus. Surprise triggered joy and brought an opportunity for memorable learning. Mary Magdalene and the disciples were utterly surprised by the appearance of the risen Jesus, even though Jesus had been preparing for this moment over the previous three years. The element of surprise reinforced this moment of joy.
- **Complete engagement**. Peter was completely caught up in the moment when Jesus began to wash the disciples' feet. He was not detached from that event, but threw himself into it. Mary Magdalene and the disciples were completely engaged in their discussion with the risen Christ: nothing was more important to them. Because of their joy, they were perhaps more ready to be commissioned than if their hearts had been low.
- **Few words**. None of these conversations were long. Jesus used just one word when he spoke to Mary and four words, 'Peace be with you', when he spoke to the disciples. The brevity did not detract from the joy of the conversations; it enhanced the impact.
- **Show the joy**. Peter was uninhibited in wanting Jesus to wash his hands and head as well as his feet. The disciples were completely 'overjoyed' in their conversation with the risen Jesus.
- **The importance of pictures and stories**. The power of the joyful conversation between Jesus and Peter was enhanced by the action of washing the feet and the drama of the whole event. For Mary Magdalene and the disciples it was the very moving picture of the living Christ that provided the drama for their joyful conversations.

- **Treasure the moment**. Imagine the strength of the simple but clear words of Jesus: 'Unless I wash you, you have no part with me', 'Mary', and 'Peace be with you.' Treasuring the moment would not have been hard.
- **Create the memories**. These conversations were so deeply embedded in the memories of the disciples that they were written in the Gospels in a remarkably fresh and lively way.
- **Turn joy into action**. Joy for Peter was wanting his hands and head to be washed as well. Jesus stretched the joy of the disciples into sending them out to be leaders of the new church.

These themes may well have been part of your most joyful conversations too. Can you list those conversation? Some of the most joyful conversations in my life include the following:

- After the birth of each of our three children the utter joy in conversations with my wife, Frances, the nurses and then later with family members.
- Strong memories of joyful conversations with each of our children in their late teens, when they had been abroad and returned after an absence. The joy of being reunited was so powerful.
- Special moments of joyful conversation with people released from pain. Their relief at having left physical or emotional pain behind released them from the baggage of months or years and led them to a whole new level of conversation.
- Long walks with friends, moving in and out of conversations ranging from the trivial to the very personal.

What are the characteristics of your list of joyful conversations? How easily can you recreate those moments with different people, so that joyful conversations are not rare things of the past but a regular part of your life?

Surprise

I cannot overstate the importance of surprise in joyful conversations. The surprise of a bunch of flowers, a new book or a hug can produce a spontaneous joyful conversation. One of C. S. Lewis's famous books was entitled *Surprised by Joy*. One of our roles in conversation can be to use surprise as a means of creating joy. We must also be ready to be surprised ourselves and allow that to be a joyful moment.

Engagement

A youth worker friend talks of the joy of conversations with young people when they are fully engaged. It may be a lively joyful conversation about sport, or it may be an intense joyful conversation about their journey of faith. As he prepares young people for baptism or confirmation, he has often had joyful conversations which have led to a new awareness and clarity of faith. This has been a special joy for both my friend and the young people.

I talked about joyful conversations to a group of university students. They identified their most joyful conversations as ones where they were fully engaged. Many were late at night when they were relaxed and involved in putting the world to rights. They enjoyed the bounce and liveliness of each other's company. The topic was less important than the sense of debate or fun. I asked what the key ingredients of success were in their conversations. They told me it was the coffee, a relaxed atmosphere and a sense of mutual support.

For these students good conversations were based on getting to know people well and feeling their support. It mattered a lot to them that their friends from college came and supported them when they played football or took part in a drama production or sang in a concert. That sense of mutual support was the bedrock of their friendships. Cradled within those friendships was the quality of conversations that would shape the future of their lives.

These young people did not just refer to conversations with their fellow students. The availability and cheerfulness of the domestic bursar and the director of works were also important. Both of these people were cheerful, open and teasing in their approach. The students could have grown-up conversations with them. They knew that if they misbehaved or were slothful they would get teased or even spoken to quite severely. The passion that these two people have for the success of the college shines through and means that conversations with students are rooted in the strength of shared endeavour.

The students commented particularly on conversations with the principal. He was 45 years older than them, but frequently joined them in the bar. He listened, he remembered what they were doing, he shared his experience with a light touch. Their main picture of the principal was of him serving them coffee and speaking brightly and cheerfully with them about any subject they chose.

The students were very positive about the college. The

quality of the joyful conversations they had there was vitally important to them. They felt encouraged and enriched. The conversations were sometimes stretching intellectually, sometimes compassionate in their concern; on other occasions they were teasing and enabling them to do things they did not particularly want to do, and at other times they were just plain fun. They were developing all the skills of effective joyful conversation. How did I know? They were just brilliant with me in responding to my questions.

Some of the most joyful conversations have very few words. A friend said that the best joyful conversation she ever had was when her son phoned her and said, 'A boy, 7lb 5oz. Bye.' When a student celebrates a successful result, there are many brief joyful conversations which will often involve just the words 'Well done' or smiles or hugs. Often very few words are needed.

Many of us are very reserved and perhaps do not show our joy as much as we could. Often we are so preoccupied with helping our children to achieve and develop in new ways that we fail to capture those moments of joy when they feel that they have moved on. We may limit our joy to the big events, when there are actually many daily developments and experiences which also need that sense of joyful reflection. There is a danger of being trite and routine, but maybe it is important to ask ourselves each day if we have had a joyful conversation with our children or with the people with whom we share our days. The older we get, perhaps the more conscious we become about the importance of showing joy. Short, joyful, intimate conversations – where the depth of our heart is open – are of immense significance. At these moments we may be vulnerable, but the benefit is potentially enormous. The affirmation given in these short joyful conversations can be very strong and can engender special trust and new confidence.

Pictures and stories

At family gatherings joyful memories can be brought to life by sharing pictures and stories. We all have our litanies of amusing stories from childhood. Shared stories at Christmas will often include scenes from Christmases past. They may be well known and often retold, but that does not detract from the joy of recapturing the emotions of happy occasions.

Many of the best conversations with children are full of pictures and stories. The joy, the honesty and the freshness are what bring us up short in these conversations. A mother recently told me of a fun conversation she had with her 5-year-old.

Nathan, out walking with his mum, looked up in delight at the moon. 'What's it doing there?' he said.

She replied, 'It looks like it's just sitting there.'

'No,' asserted Nathan, 'there are no chairs.'

His mum commented, 'Well, I would say it's hanging there, but there's no rope either.'

Nathan and his mum painted different pictures in their minds about the moon. Perhaps in this gentle, joyful banter they were reflecting that everything is not what it seems.

Engaging with children is a wonderful way of keeping spontaneous and fresh in conversation. I had a wonderfully animated conversation with a 10-year-old recently. He enjoyed his school and especially the sport. I asked him what conversations were special at school. He said, 'I don't really talk to the teachers, I listen to what they say. I talk with my friends about football, about what's happening at school and about rock music.'

'What sort of rock music?' I asked.

'Oh, rock music between 1967 and 1973.'

I nearly said, 'But you weren't alive then,' but I thought that if I did, he would look askance and think I was rather stupid. So we had a lively, engaging conversation about this period of rock music history.

He also brightly told me that he and his friends had a lot of conversations about jokes. He said, 'I enjoy chatting to my friends.' Then a look of boredom crossed his face, but his eyes lit up again as he said, 'I'm going to play football outside with my brother!' And off he went, chatting away to his brother about who was going to kick the ball first.

The boy's grandmother came over and asked if I had needed rescuing. 'No,' I said, 'talking to a 10-year-old is so special.' There is a freshness and a joy in both their words and their eyes. For them life is good and new and exciting: the boring bits of conversation need not last too long, because there is always football to be played in the garden.

Treasure the moment

The joy of conversations is enhanced by treasuring the moment and reliving it. One New Year's Day we were in San Francisco and kept riding on the streetcars. The streetcar attendants were so cheerful and the journeys such fun that we keep reliving the memories of those journeys and the joyful conversations we had.

The son of a neighbour has become an internationally

acclaimed musician as part of the Medici Quartet. None of the fame takes away from his joy in making music or the joy of talking with him after he has given a performance. He treasures the moments from a recital that has flowed, talking joyfully about the experience of intimacy that can be found in working well as a group of four musicians.

To the extent that we hold in our minds moments of joyful conversation, we can relive them when we meet that person again. I recently met a former colleague with whom I had had no dealings for nine years. We immediately recalled some good conversations we had enjoyed and went straight into a new and positive conversation about an endeavour in which we could both be involved. It was as if the nine years had gone in a trice. What helped so much was the immediacy of remembering good moments of interchange from previous occasions.

For a number of months I helped facilitate a learning set involving people from very different cultural backgrounds. As people got to know each other they shared at a very deep level some of their aspirations and fears. One participant described the level of interchange as 'magical'. When we had our last meeting there were tears of joy as people relived some of the moments they had shared together as a group. It was vital to take time at the end to treasure those moments of joyful conversation. In doing so we created another special time of joyful conversation. This was not indulgent. The members of the group had stretched each other's thinking enormously and by the end there was a much greater awareness of the contribution brought by the perspectives of different cultures. The very act of weeping joyful tears reinforced the learning that had taken place in conversation between the different participants.

A special sequence of joyful conversations took place during a nine-day walk I undertook from Arnside to

Saltburn – right across England. I had companions on seven of the days, including my daughter, a friend from undergraduate days, a friend from postgraduate days, the father of one of my eldest son's good friends, a friend from Durham and a new work colleague. We found such richness in sharing the joy of times past, the fun of the walk and the pleasure of discussing aspirations for the future. We were sharing memories and creating new memories at the same time.

The most joyful conversations for you may happen over the dinner table, in the coffee bar, out on a walk or in the pub. Whatever is the right environment for you, the more often you are in that environment to create the context for joyful conversation, the better you will feel about life and the better you will be prepared for the range of painful and challenging conversations that will inevitably also be part of your life. I was brought up by the sea in Yorkshire. When Frances and I want to relax, we go down to the south coast and walk on the chalk cliffs of the Seven Sisters or on Seaford Head. As we walk briskly in the open air, we find that joy is released into our conversation.

Joyful conversations are often tinged with pain. I talked recently with a Zimbabwean exile who had been forced to leave his home country. He had held a senior chief executive post in Zimbabwe and now held a responsible post at a much more junior level in the UK. He was positive and determined to do well in his new world. He was joyful in his new work and accepted the reality of his situation. The pain of having to leave his home country was still there, but he had managed to contain it in such a way that he was able to enter into a new world with new joy.

Sometimes our memories of joyful conversations are just good memories of relaxed and amusing exchanges.

One of the joys of working in London is walking through the London parks. On some mornings I walk to work through St James's Park. In the middle of the park there is a delightful pedestrian bridge with a majestic view of Buckingham Palace to the west and Whitehall to the east. For me it is one of the most evocative places in London. One winter's morning there were two police officers standing on the bridge. They both looked so relaxed and nonchalant. I stopped to talk with them about what sort of conversations they had on the bridge.

They told me they stood on the bridge as a deterrent to the growing number of people who had taken to riding their bicycles through St James's Park on their way to work. I asked if they had caught anyone this morning.

'No, so the deterrent is obviously working.' They said that most of the conversations they had were with tourists asking the way. Once, standing immediately outside Buckingham Palace, a tourist had asked the police officer, 'Where is Buckingham Palace?' He resisted saying sharply, 'Immediately over my left shoulder,' and maintained his politeness throughout the exchange.

They told me that they would talk to anybody who asked them a question. They always wanted to talk in a polite, courteous and joyful way. They always had to be on their guard, however. Just occasionally they were deliberately distracted. They also had to watch for the demon cyclist out of the corner of their eye. They needed to be alert about what else was happening in the vicinity while giving focused attention to one person. One police officer told me of an occasion when he was talking intently to one person and heard the sound of metal clashing on metal. He immediately rushed off to the scene of an accident on the north side of St James's Park. There the courteous approach had to stay the same, alongside an immediate change of gear to take decisive action after the accident.

These two police officers were a wonderful example of how to be absolutely focused on the conversation in hand, while remaining alert and able to respond quickly to different situations. What could be more of a contrast than giving directions to a tourist one minute and then the next minute talking to shaken people after an accident and taking decisive action on the traffic flow? No wonder they said they received a lot of joy out of their jobs.

Next steps

How can we put into practice the principles and themes we have set out in this chapter? The guidelines below may be relevant to you in many different ways in the context of joyful conversations.

- **The importance of surprise**. Can you bring surprise into conversations more often? Not in a way that takes people aback and throws them on the defensive, but in a way that helps produce new life and energy. The benefits of pleasant surprises can often be huge. On one occasion I suggested to somebody I work with that he might surprise his wife by taking her and their grown-up children out for a meal to celebrate his transition into a new job. I got a message back from his wife saying that it had been such a joyful occasion: they had not been out as a family for a meal together for a number of years.
- **Complete engagement**. It is so easy to stand back and not be fully engaged in a conversation. We are preoccupied by other things on our mind. We are

aware of another challenging or painful conversation we are about to have. Sometimes we need to practise the art of complete engagement and try to blot out other things. Maybe the easiest type of conversation to be completely engaged in is a joyful one. You cannot experience joy in a conversation unless you are fully immersed in it.

- **Few words**. Joyful conversations are often short and result from a few words that lift or bring good cheer. It is perfectly possible to have a short joyful conversation with a ticket collector on the train or at the station. The joy here does not come from detailed intimacy but from the warmth of a brief but positive exchange. A test at the end of each day is to ask yourself how many brief positive exchanges you have had.

- **Show the joy**. Are we too inhibited sometimes? Do we hold back when it would be good to praise, to acknowledge, to say how pleased we are about something that has happened? We can show joy not just in our words but also in our smile and, where appropriate, through a gentle touch.

- **The importance of pictures and stories**. How often do we create different contexts or use visual images to illustrate joy within a conversation? We all know the expression, 'A picture tells a thousand words.' One of my colleagues keeps referring to the importance of 'using parables rather than sermons'. The more our conversations are rooted in images and pictures, the more memorable they are likely to be and the greater impact they are likely to have.

- **Treasure the moment**. Some moments pass quickly and others are very slow. We can sometimes slow the clock down and hold a moment for longer. Treasuring the good moments in joyful conversations is so important. They act as a bank of energy as we move through conversations which are challenging and painful. Treasuring the moment is about reliving them. Sometimes before a difficult meeting it can be helpful to hold in your mind a good moment when you were both relaxed and engaged. That can prepare you in a special way for a difficult conversation. Holding onto treasured moments can simply recreate joy through a sense of thoughtfulness. Sharing them can create a new joyful conversation.

- **Create the memories**. Try to define the type of occasions when your conversations are at their most joyful, be it around the dining table, on a walk, after church or in a pub. If those contexts help generate joyful conversations for you, hold on to that experience and try to recreate those occasions at regular intervals. This is not about being selfish, it is about being self-aware and knowing how best to create positive memories. When each of our children reached the age of 18, we gave them a large album which included photographs from the first 18 years of their life and poems or stories they had written and pictures they had painted. This was a feast of good memories which we often relive with them. There are many benefits in creating and reliving a set of good memories to recreate a wealth of joyful conversations.

- **Turn joy into action**. Moments of joy can provide the springboard for action. In family discussions times of joy can give a sense of unity which provides a basis for taking difficult decisions affecting the future. In a voluntary organization or church, moments of joy can provide the context for moving on in a positive way and for deciding on bold next steps.

Questions for reflection

1. What would your emotions have been if you had been Peter and Jesus had asked to wash your feet?
2. What would it have felt like to have been in the shoes of Mary Magdalene and the disciples meeting with the risen Christ?
3. What have been some of your most joyful moments?
4. How important is surprise in generating joyful conversations?
5. How might you take forward some of the principles about joyful conversations identified in this chapter?
6. How might you show more joy in conversations?
7. What for you is the best context in which to generate and embrace joyful conversations?
8. How might you turn joyful conversations into fruitful action about next steps?

Practical principles and pitfalls

9

We have looked at various types of conversations. In each chapter we have started with two conversations that Jesus had and identified key themes or principles relevant for each type of conversation. This chapter draws together some key principles for successful conversations and then looks at the pitfalls to watch. These are not definitive lists: they are prompts for further reflection.

In the first chapter I referred to three overriding characteristics of the way Jesus approached conversations. He was focusing on *engagement*, *discernment* and *stretching*. These three principles are evident throughout each of the seven different types of conversations that we have considered.

First principle: engagement

This covers the basis for a conversation in terms of trust, confidentiality and openness. It is also about how we interact, covering silence and stillness, humour, communion and how we travel together.

- **Trust**. The crucial umbrella for any conversation that is going to go beyond the purely factual is trust. Trust may be based on a long friendship or acquaintance. On other occasions trust has to be established immediately. Ideally, assume trust is there until it is broken. When it is broken, talk it through and rebuild it. Do not assume that trust can never be recreated.
- **Confidentiality**. The confidentiality rules are crucial. Often in short conversations there is no issue about confidentiality. But on other occasions the confidentiality arrangements must be absolutely clear and both parties must be secure within them.
- **Openness**. There are some territories we do not want to expose even to our best friend. But the more open people are with each other the richer a conversation is likely to be. Part of starting a serious conversation is a mutual understanding about the degree of openness that there will be. There are bound to be occasions in negotiating conversations where there cannot be complete openness. But the further the boundaries can be pushed in the direction of openness, the more successful conversations are likely to be.
- **Silence and stillness**. Silence gives a chance for people to think, and possibly change their point of view. The main turning points in conversation will often be those moments of stillness. We undermine our own aspirations in conversation if we do not leave stillness both for ourselves and the people with whom we are speaking. Some conversations are entirely silent. To share stillness and silence with someone can speak oceans of love and understanding where words are irrelevant. On the other hand, silent conversations where the tension is palpable can speak of enmity and hostility. Sometimes conversations with no words need

to stay that way. Sometimes, however, especially when the silence means hostility, some attempt at breaking that silence is worth the risk.

- **Face to face**. Ideally conversations are face to face. It is the exchange through the eyes that adds so much to the words. Being physically present with somebody enables you to understand their perspective more clearly. It allows warmth and challenge to flow more easily. When there has been a strong face-to-face relationship, however, phone conversations can be just as effective. You can learn to read silences and breath sounds on the phone almost as quickly as you can interpret somebody's eyes. Phone conversations can work powerfully even when there has been no face-to-face contact. I recently spent 90 minutes on the phone preparing someone for interview whom I had not previously met. It worked well, but we needed to spend a few minutes at the start just getting to know each other and talking informally before getting down to the serious business.

- **Humour**. This is powerful in conversations. If two people can see the same funny side of an issue, they are likely to be looking in the same direction and be willing to learn from each other. When you are talking with somebody, how can you best make them smile? This is perhaps the most important question when beginning a conversation with a new person. It is not about sharing jokes but about what makes someone's eyes light up. Sometimes early on in conversations it is worth asking the question, 'What makes you smile?' 'What is it that you really enjoy about this area of work or this place?'

- **Travelling together**. The more a conversation can be a shared journey of discovery, the more satisfying it is likely to be. One context that often works for conversations is when two people walk together. It may be a lunchtime walk with a colleague through a London park or the streets of New York. It might be a walk through the hills at a weekend. That sense of travelling together can produce shared insights. When somebody is in difficulty and wants to share in conversation, it helps when we are clear in our words that we are walking on their journey too.

- **Communion**. The best conversations often happen when people are eating or drinking together. One of the most powerful of Jesus' conversations was between Jesus and his disciples at the Last Supper shortly before his crucifixion. Many of us can remember crucial meals we shared with our family and friends at key moments in our lives, and the conversations remain richly embedded in our minds. Part of the start of a conversation is often a cup of tea or a glass of water. As families, eating together often provides the one context where we all sit down and share in conversation. Sometimes we are not bold enough in inviting people to share a meal or a cup of coffee with us. Creating that space for communion is rarely wasted.

- **Space**. In busy diaries, leaving adequate space for conversations is important. This is not always easy. When teenagers want to talk, it is generally at the time of their choosing (which may well be 11 o'clock at night). Forcing the issue about talking through crucial issues with teenagers at moments of your own choosing is hardly ever going to work.

- **Flexibility**. Good creative conversations do not just happen to order. Patricia Shaw, in her book *Changing Conversations in Organisations*, advocates the prolonged coffee break as a self-organizing type of ordinary conversation where people can have a sequence of creative conversations in an unstructured way. Her thesis is that any dynamic organization results from lively conversations between individuals, and it is therefore essential to create the space and rationale for those conversations to take place. Her presumption is that the activity of conversation itself is the key process through which forms of organizing are dynamically sustained and changed. To be healthy, any organization, be it a family, a community, a church or a business, needs the flexibility to let conversations flower and be creative.

Second principle: discernment

Discernment is about the way we approach conversations. It is about clarity, good questions, experimentation, a willingness to learn, modesty, curiosity and the willingness to take risks.

- **Clarity**. It helps to enter most conversations with clarity about their purpose. That purpose might be to encourage or to raise somebody's spirits. It might be just to have a factual exchange in a positive and cheerful way. On other occasions the purpose will be more complicated. A conversation might be part of a difficult sequence of exchanges. But the clearer we are at the start about the scope of the conversation, the easier it is for that conversation to be enjoyable and productive.
- **Questions**. The best questions are not closed, leading to just 'yes' or 'no' answers. The best questions open up issues and enable people to clarify their own thinking. The 'why' questions which press somebody to be clear

about his or her own perspective can help to clarify self-understanding. The best questions are asked without judgement and give people the freedom to be honest with themselves and with you.

- **Curiosity**. Keeping your curiosity is crucial in conversations. Understanding why something is important to someone else gives such a clear insight into their perspective. Try standing in the shoes of the person to whom you are talking. Think about why they are wearing what they are wearing. Why are they talking about these particular issues? The more you think 'inside' somebody, the more interesting their perspective in conversation becomes. Curiosity might have killed the cat, but it enlivens conversations. In *Turning to One Another*, Margaret Wheatley says, 'We will succeed in changing this world only if we think and work together in new ways. We don't have to let go of what we believe, but we do need to be curious about what someone else believes.'

- **Experimentation**. We are all creatures of habit. We probably follow similar patterns in the way in which we converse with others. It is worth observing yourself and seeing the approach you use. Might it be worth sometimes taking a different approach? If you generally take a reflective approach, perhaps on some occasions you could experiment with coming in earlier in a conversation with a proposition. As we experiment and widen our repertoire of approaches, the impact for good that we have in conversations can grow.

- **Risk**. The best conversations occur when individuals risk sharing something of themselves. It might also involve taking a risk in terms of putting forward a particular perspective. This will lead to greater understanding about each other's approach and about the relevant counterarguments.

- **Brevity**. If you find yourself talking too much or repeating yourself, there must be a question mark about how well the conversation is working. If you are talking quite a bit but flowing and the person with whom you are talking is fully engaged, then to keep talking may well be absolutely the right thing to do. Brevity is sometimes what is needed, however, particularly to help somebody draw out key points.

Third principle: stretching

Quality conversations are not only engaging and discerning, they also stretch the participants. Stretching is about allowing learning to take place, enabling conversations to be dynamic, transcending boundaries, challenging and providing an effective means to reach a conclusion. The conversations of Jesus built on engagement and discernment, but virtually always led to stretching the thinking of those with whom he was talking.

- **Dynamic**. If you can predict the end of a conversation, you may be boxing it in. It is right to have a focus on the sort of outcomes that might result from a conversation, but if we restrict those outcomes too much we are putting blinkers around our own thinking. If we go into conversations saying we are not sure what the outcome will be, we can enjoy the surprise of seeing conversations move into new and different territories. One of the great joys of working as a coach is that you never know where each conversation will end up. That is part of the richness of the job.

- **Debate**. A formal debate is a distinct form of conversation. As two people debate an issue in parliament or in congress, there is often a frankness of expression. Too often there is also rigidity. But in the best of debates there is a keenness to deploy the key facts and a willingness to learn and modify one's position. Part of healthy conversation is debate. Working through differences is crucial. There is a time and place to be frank about differences. A sequence of conversations that always put the most difficult issues aside are not likely to grow in the same depth and quality as other conversations which include a healthy element of debate.

- **Transcending boundaries**. Some of the most interesting conversations come when the participants are from different ages, cultures, personal circumstances and faiths. Deliberately looking for differences and enjoying those differences can make conversations a very bonding experience. There is something very special about conversations between grandparents and grandchildren which transcend age and personal circumstances. Many of our organizations do not encourage quality conversations to take place between people of markedly different perspectives. Many clubs and societies only bring together people with a similar perspective. Churches may well be one of the few institutions that bring together people from very varied backgrounds into quite intimate relationships. Churches are in a privileged position in that they are able to encourage conversations between people with widely different backgrounds and views.

- **Varying speed**. Conversations have their own speed. Sometimes they flow quickly and at other times slowly.

I am very conscious when coaching that sometimes two hours can fly by and just occasionally those hours can feel like eternity. That is a good moment for me to ask myself why a conversation is dragging: is it something to do with my own level of engagement? If we sense that a conversation is going slowly, it is right to ask if we can do anything to change the situation. Maybe we need to move to a new topic, or maybe it is time for another round of coffee.

- **Challenge**. In conversations between people who know each other well there is always the scope for challenge. If conversations are becoming too comfortable or inward looking, a challenge can focus attention effectively. It may be a challenging comment from a GP about how somebody is looking after him- or herself. It may be at certain moments in family life. It may be easiest to do in a work context, where the robustness of challenge is part of the accepted routine. Sometimes challenge has to be done very carefully if it is not to produce a defensive reaction. Done badly, it can be very counterproductive. The best way to learn is through experimentation and ensuring careful feedback.

- **Freshness**. One of the most influential books I have read in recent years is *How to Start a Creative Revolution at Work* by the What If team. They put a strong emphasis on 'freshness' in any type of organization. The authors say that we often have standard routines in conversation when we really need to bring freshness. We need to find alternative ways of describing or experiencing an issue or problem. If we focus on breaking patterns in the way we talk and think about issues, we can create a freshness that will raise our sights. Faced with an invitation to meet new people or an opportunity to try something different, the logic of the pattern-breaker is, 'I'm not sure I'm going to enjoy this. Good, I'll do it anyway.' Trying to bring freshness and express things differently can stretch our conversations to be more productive.

- **Compelling modesty**. This enables us to understand where people are coming from and be more convincing about the next steps we suggest. In his book *From Good to Great* Jim Collins looks at a range of different types of organizations to identify what has made them particularly successful. His overriding themes are that successful leaders have shown 'unwavering resolve' and 'compelling modesty'. The compelling modesty theme is about listening and learning all the time: listening to customers, partners and the people with whom we work. Unwavering resolve is about our clarity of direction, having taken very careful account of the results of conversations with those affected.
- **A means to an end**. Good conversation is enjoyable in itself. But conversation is part of a process which, in one way or another, is moving towards affirmation or conclusion. Conversation with young children has a value in itself in terms of them learning the skills of conversation. Even here these learning conversations are part of the richness that can be found in building relationships and the ability to share and converse with others.

Most conversations will have elements of engagement, discernment and stretching. Above all, a good conversation needs to be fit for its purpose. I received some very clear views about conversation recently from the secretary of a very senior figure. She talked regularly with a range of people in the organization. She was not overly impressed by their management or communication skills. What makes a real difference, she said, is if they smile not only with their mouth but also with their eyes. Her main concern was with people who rambled. For her a good short conversation was cheerful and direct. If a point needs to be made, it should be made directly and a conclusion reached. Rambling on too much when you are trying to organize the diary or move business on is a distraction. She readily accepted that in other contexts an open-ended conversation can be great – but it still needs to be fit for its purpose. If you are trying to sort out the diary, words should not be wasted, practical constraints should be clear, with a conversation designed to reach a conclusion that everyone can live with. I empathized with her positive approach, but felt sad for her frustration that her ideal was so often out of reach.

To conclude this section, here are two wonderful quotes from Samuel Johnson about 'fit for purpose' conversations:

This is the happiest conversation where there is no competition, no vanity, but a calm quiet interchange of sentiments.

John Wesley's conversation is good but he is never at leisure, he is always obliged to go at a certain hour. This is very disagreeable to a man who loves to fold his legs and have out his talk as I do.

My sympathies would be with John Wesley, who, after a certain time, clearly had better things to do!

Pitfalls to watch

With the best will in the world, we can all be caught in different pitfalls. We can easily believe that words make all the difference, we can be inconsistent, we may be too influenced by initial impressions, we might not allow for changing phases in conversations or be sensitive enough to cross-cultural comparisons. We need to watch for the danger signals of conversations becoming too one-sided.

Words do not make all the difference

The words we use are only part of the story. Albert Mehrabian published some landmark research in 1981 measuring the impact of voice tone and body language on our perception of trustworthiness. This showed that if what you are saying and what you are doing conflict, people are most likely to take the message from the body language (what you are doing) as more significant. Here is what Mehrabian found:

- Fifty-three per cent of the impression we make on another person comes from our behaviour and body language – the way we act, move, gesture and express ourselves and the tone and inflection of our voice; whether we are confident, organized and interested; whether we fumble around, are nervous or distracted; whether the meaning or point of our message is clear or muddled.
- Forty per cent of the impression we make comes from who we are. This involves our credibility and confidence. Are we likeable, funny, or interesting? Do they like us?

- Seven per cent of the impression we make comes from the actual words we say. This includes the content of what we are saying as well as the choice of words.

This is a salutary warning that our body language can so easily over-rule our words. In conversation it is not just our words that matter, it is our whole being and approach. This research reinforces the importance of building trust as soon as possible in any conversation and demonstrating complete engagement in that conversation.

Watch inconsistency

It is easy to fall into the trap of inconsistency without realizing it. Inevitably we are affected by our moods. Sometimes we will be more willing to talk to people than on other occasions.

If we change our pattern of conversation we can so easily create suspicions or unfounded worries. When I had a very busy period I did not engage with some of my colleagues as much as I normally do. I was preoccupied, but some of my colleagues thought I was being distant and was in some way withdrawing from them. I was challenged about this and recognized that I had not been very approachable. The lesson to me was that I gave off negative signals without realizing I was doing so. Once we set a pattern in the way we converse with people, they will be very observant of the way we change that pattern. If we close up, it produces suspicion. If we open up, there may be surprise but also pleasure.

Beware initial impressions

It is often easy to make a hasty judgement about an individual. Many successful leaders pride themselves on being able to make accurate initial assessments of individuals. This attitude, however, can border on the arrogant and can write off people who might initially simply have been nervous at meeting a senior figure. Whatever the initial impression, at the start of a conversation the ideal is to reserve judgement, particularly if that initial impression has been critical.

A colleague was camping close to the Grand Canyon. It was time to walk back to the campsite. It was very dark. Eventually he saw a small camp fire burning in the distance with a couple of men sitting around it. He shouted, 'I'm lost!' Immediately the two men jumped up and ran in the opposite direction. Then they stopped. One man said, 'Bears don't talk.' Rather sheepishly, the two campers then welcomed my lost friend and pointed him in the right direction. The campers told themselves that next time they heard a plaintive cry of 'I'm lost!' they would not run away. We all run the risk of writing off lost souls as 'bears' if we give too much weight to initial false impressions.

Allow for changing phases

The best conversations move through a variety of different phases and do not get stuck in one particular phase. They will move from reflection to debate, from the immediate to the long term. In the richest relationships the conversations will move across work and personal boundaries.

Allow yourself to be surprised about the dynamic way in which conversations move. A friend told me of a wonderful conversation in three parts which oscillated between very direct challenge and companionship. My friend was on a train journey in France. He was sitting in a compartment in which a French couple were talking heatedly about English attitudes. These people did not know that my friend was English and understood French fluently. My friend could not resist joining in and a heated debate ensued about French and British attitudes. After 20 minutes of acrimonious discussion the French man's wife said, 'Enough!' and got out the food hamper. All was sweetness and joy as they shared bread and wine. They talked about all that was best in the Anglo-French relationship as they enjoyed a wonderful picnic with excellent wine and cheerful conversation.

Eventually the food was put way and the challenging conversation was renewed. It was different now, however, because they had shared a meal together. The difference was that now the challenging conversation involved humour. The language was just as strong, the arguments just as forceful, but it was within a context of companionship rather than aggression. The fact that they had eaten together, sharing bread and wine, made such a difference. The conversation following that communion had all the robustness of the first conversation, but it was now cemented in good friendship. The best challenging conversations are often part of the changing pattern of a relationship which allows the rigour of debate to be set within the context of a bond of friendship.

Cross-cultural comparisons

The cultural background is so important in the context of conversation. A friend was born in the Philippines and now works in the UK. In his home culture conversations were much more deferential than in the Western world. Social hierarchy was important. You did not challenge your elders and betters. Any relationship needed to be based first on building mutual support with lots of humour before there could be the possibility of a challenging conversation. My friend's explanation was that a long history of colonial influence had brought about a deferential attitude to authority.

A friend with a Punjabi heritage who has lived in the UK all his life tells me of the very strong respect in his tradition for people older than oneself. The result is an unwillingness to challenge one's elders, even if what they really need is strong leadership from younger people in the community who have had the benefit of a high level of education and a wider perspective. Coming from a culture in which you do not really look people in the eye until you know them well, my friend has not found it easy to develop the Western approach of early strong eye contact which is both warm and challenging.

The Dutch and the Germans are brought up to expect challenge in conversation. A Dutch friend explains that because the Dutch language does not have such a variety of words as some other languages, conversation tends to be focused and direct. For him a good conversation is robust, with strong views expressed. As he lives in the UK, this approach has got him into difficulties on a number of occasions: he is very conscious that he needs to modify his approach to fit the cultural context.

One of the great joys of the twenty-first century is

increased multicultural and international awareness. Talking with people from different cultures brings a variety of perspective that is so enriching. But a clear understanding of how conversation works in different cultures is crucial to ensuring effective multicultural working. These cultural differences are particularly important when it comes to conversations that are challenging. The person who does not look you in the eye may be demonstrating the good practice with which she was brought up. It is not that she is being shifty. The person who is too robust may well be reflecting his own cultural background.

One-sided conversations

In the best conversations there is a genuine interchange between two people. This may not mean that they each do 50 per cent of the talking: one person may be sharing in some detail which the other responds briefly through questions or short reflections. One-sided conversations often occur when one party is 'rattling on' with no awareness of the other person's boredom or lack of interest. If your mind begins to wander, this is an indicator that the conversation is not fully engaging both parties. That may be the moment to deliberately try to re-engage through a question or reflection.

Sometimes when a conversation becomes one-sided, the sooner it is ended the better. Otherwise the participants will be reluctant to engage in a further attempt at creative conversation.

Successful conversations can be messy

Margaret Wheatley's book *Turning to One Another* suggests that the best conversations depend on our willingness to forget about clear categories. She writes,

> Because conversation is the natural way that humans think together, it is, like all life, messy. Life doesn't move in straight lines and neither does a good conversation. When a conversation begins, people always say things that don't connect.

She argues that we often try to make connections when sometimes it is important to let go of that impulse and just sit with the messiness. We have to be willing to listen and curious about the diversity of experiences. She summarizes so effectively the value of allowing spontaneity in conversation.

> When we are brave enough to risk a conversation, we have the chance to rediscover what it means to be human. In conversation we practise good humour and behaviour. We think, we laugh, we cry, we tell stories of our day. We become visible to one another. We gain insights and new understandings. Conversation wakes us up. We no longer accept being treated poorly. We become people who work to change our situation.

Conclusion: 10
Where next?

Lewis Carroll wrote, 'What is the use of a book ... without pictures or conversations?' The aim of this book is to prompt conversations. These may be conversations in your head or with a range of different people. Why are conversations so important to us?

- It is through conversations that we define who we are and what matters to us.
- Conversations are about how we connect with others.
- Conversations offer us a chance to share and to clarify our purpose.
- They provide a context for fun, curiosity and adventure.
- Conversations are enriched by variety: thoughtfulness, laughter, challenge and encouragement are all important.
- Quietness in conversation provides a place for calmness within our key relationships.
- Conversation is crucial in the way we relate to each other and in our relationship with God.
- All conversations begin with a willingness to listen.

The Gospels are full of conversations that Jesus had. His impact on others came through those conversations. Some were happy and some very sad. Others were clearly challenging. Looking at the range of conversations Jesus had illustrates how much store he set on relationships with those he met. The role model of Jesus provides a framework for conversation that is engaging, discerning and stretching.

Michael Schluter, writing in the Winter 2004 edition of *Engage*, talks of Christianity as a 'relational' religion. This means that 'getting relationships right, or putting them right, is of greater significance than increasing national or personal wealth'. He writes, 'People are much more likely to understand the biblical message, the significance of Jesus and the forgiveness he offers, if they have learnt to see the world in relational terms.' It is the quality of our conversations that builds the relationships which are so essential for emotional and spiritual growth.

Conversations are at their best when they are both purposeful and full of fun, curiosity and adventure. I have a former colleague, Barry, who has a wonderful Northern Ireland brogue. Now living in Edinburgh, he ran businesses in the United States for many years. His take on conversations is very clear. Remember, he says, 7 per cent of the message is in the words, 40 per cent in the tone and 53 per cent is the visual impact. He uses an approach in conversations which he bases on the word 'magic'.

M: Make contact.
A: Act positively.
G: Get to the heart of the matter.
I: Interpret the facts.
C: Close with agreement.

He enjoys the magic of conversations in not knowing where they are leading while being purposeful in taking them forward. Making contact is about identifying ways of building encouragement. Using a person's name is crucial. Acting positively is about showing that you understand or can help. He uses the example of a taxi driver. You feel so different when the taxi driver responds positively by saying he knows the way to your destination. Contrast your feelings when there is a furrowed brow from your driver.

Barry quotes the Scandinavian Airlines phrase, 'The first contact is the moment of truth.' Getting to the heart of the matter is central to Barry's approach. In ad hoc conversations part of the skill is in identifying informal short agendas very quickly. Sometimes these are explicitly agreed and at other times they are simply in your own head. For Barry there is a special delight in defining very quickly the one or two things about which it would be good to reach a conclusion with someone you meet in passing. The initial polite contact and engagement makes it easier to move to the heart of the matter.

Interpreting the facts involves making sure you understand the key issues, possibly by playing them back. 'Am I right about the key issue here?' or, 'Can I just check my understanding of this?' A crucial question for Barry at the end of each impromptu conversation concerns the agreement or understanding that has been reached. Sometimes there is a precise conclusion; at other times there is just a shared acceptance of a view or an approach.

Barry's wonderfully disciplined approach shows the value of entering a conversation with a clear view of the main theme and not getting too bogged down in the detail. Have the parameters clear in your mind, while letting the magic of the conversation flow. Barry says it is a bit like doing a jigsaw: you set out the four corners first and let the detail take care of itself. Sometimes, though, we only know one corner, and we have to let the conversation flow for a while until trust is built up before it is clear where the other three corners are.

The excitement of conversation lies in its fun, its curiosity and the sense of adventure. But it is also about quietness and stillness. Sometimes there are particular places where we enjoy conversation most. Sometimes there are places of stillness that help us be creative as we think through the conversations we want to have.

For many people conversations are not only with each other but also with God. Sometimes these are conversations which we fill with words, but sometimes they involve no words at all. Sometimes structured prayers are helpful, bringing the richness of our heritage of language. On other occasions unstructured and informal prayers bring us close to a sense of God's presence. Some people choose to use particular approaches in order to practise 'the presence of God' and to enter into conversation with awe and reverence. For some these conversations are best led by one person as part of a congregation; for others the best approach is a private conversation in a private place.

The importance of all conversations with God is that they should be two-way, with a time of listening rather than 'talking at' God. Mother Teresa was once being interviewed by a journalist about her life and faith. At one point the interviewer asked her what she said to God when she prayed. 'I don't say anything,' she replied. 'I just listen.'

'And when you listen,' said the interviewer, 'what does God say?'

'He doesn't say anything,' she replied. 'He just listens.' Before the bewildered journalist could say anything more, she added, 'And if you don't understand that, I can't explain it to you.'

The picture of Mother Teresa and God silently listening to each other is a powerful one. That is sometimes what quiet reflection is about: in a conversation with no words we become more at peace with ourselves and the next steps in our lives. As we talk to each other we engage creatively, but sometimes, when we sit in each other's presence with no words, we are just as creative as we share in that special bond of friendship.

I hope this book has helped to bring you to an increased awareness of the importance of conversations, and I hope it has stimulated you to think about how you can use conversations all the more effectively. Enjoy all those conversations in store for you, whether they are listening, encouraging, challenging, short, painful, unresponsive or joyful. A world that is too busy for conversation has forgotten how to live. In your conversations allow yourself to be fully engaged, try to bring discernment and let yourself be stretched. Conversation is a priceless gift: enjoy it.

Notes for small groups

These notes are designed to help people facilitating small group discussions based on the seven types of conversations illustrated in this book.

Chapters 2 to 8 provide a starting point for small group discussions. Each concludes with a list of potential questions as a basis for discussion. The overarching principles in Chapter 9 might provide a basis for summary discussion at the end of the session about joyful conversations (Chapter 8), or it could be a separate concluding discussion.

The starting point for the small group discussion could be:

- the two passages from the Gospels given at the start of each chapter, *or*
- specific examples from individual members of the group about a conversation or conversations that fit the relevant category.

If your chosen starting point is the two passages from the Gospels, it would still be worth asking people to contribute some examples early on in the discussion.

Each of the seven chapters aims to identify themes from Jesus' conversations that are relevant more widely. The person leading the discussion could draw out those themes, illustrating them from the stories of Jesus and from their own experience, and could then use those themes as the basis for discussion.

An advantage of having a series of discussions on conversations is that it allows individuals to reflect between meetings about the conversations they have had. It also enables participants to think about how they are going to experiment between one discussion and the next.

First small group meeting on listening conversations

The advantage of the first discussion being on listening conversations is that it provides an opportunity for members of the group to:

- reflect on what listening means;
- consider how good a listener they are;
- experiment with listening during the small group session;
- reflect on how they are going to try out some listening skills over the succeeding week;
- consider how they are going to experiment in the conversations they will have.

The chapter on listening conversations includes some practical approaches to listening which could be tried out within the group. These cover three experiments with people working in pairs.

- Both speak simultaneously for 30 seconds about a particular topic.
- One person acts as a listener and takes up the position of a rock (no eye contact, no movement, no sound). The other person speaks for about a minute about the things they enjoy about their job or their weekend activities. After a minute, the two participants switch roles and repeat.
- One person acts as a listener, but this time is free to use normal eye contact and body language, but no words, only encouraging sounds (i.e. 'um', 'ah', 'hm'). The other person speaks for about a minute on the things they find difficult about their job or their responsibilities in the community or the church. After a minute, the two participants switch roles and repeat.

After these discussions the participants are asked:

- How easy was it to listen?
- How easy was it to speak?
- What were the learning points?

Another practical exercise in listening skills is for people to split into pairs. Each person is asked to talk briefly about something that is very important to them. The other person should just ask questions and make no comment. The discussion goes on for about 15 minutes and then the two participants swap their roles. Each person should aim to listen intently and ask questions that encourage the speaker to develop their thoughts further. The comments should not be criticism or parallel points, but just questions. Participants are then asked to comment on what it felt like to be fully listened to in this sort of way. Then they have a chance to reflect on how they could adopt that approach more effectively in their day-to-day lives.

If these sorts of questions are used successfully as experiments in the group discussion about listening skills, it is possible to apply some of the learning in future meetings.

Subsequent discussions

Each subsequent discussion could start with the following refresher questions.

- What have you particularly remembered about the way Jesus engaged in that particular type of conversation?
- What practical pictures about conversations have stayed with you since the last meeting?
- In what ways have you been able to experiment with using different approaches in conversations?
- What have your particular learning points been since the last discussion?

In addition, at the end of each small group discussion participants could be invited to reflect on the following questions.

- What has struck you most about the conversations Jesus had in that particular category?
- What are the learning points you want to take forward into the forthcoming week?
- What are you going to experiment with over the next week?
- How will you know whether some of the approaches

you use have worked? What feedback arrangements will you use?

Below are some other approaches that can help make the discussion come alive.

- Read the two passages from the Gospels as if they were a conversation, by asking different people to take on the roles of Jesus, other characters in the story and the narrator.
- Invite somebody to enact a relevant conversation that has been very important to him or her.
- Invite people to experiment with different sorts of body language in the way they talk or listen.
- Invite people to keep a diary of key conversations over the period of the meetings, possibly listing their conversations under the seven different categories.

Final meeting

The final meeting could combine the discussion on joyful conversations with a general recap and look forward. Or it could involve a recap and look forward based on the general principles given in Chapter 9. As you recap the different types of conversation, participants might be asked to suggest:

- a particular learning point from each type of conversation;
- what types of conversations they want to experiment with;

- how they will know whether they have been successful.

They could also be invited to reflect on whether their experience is in line with the overarching themes in Chapter 9. Below are some approaches you might take.

- Which of the overarching themes are most important?
- Are you surprised by the importance you now attach to some of these principles?
- Which pitfalls are you most concerned about?
- What are you now going to do differently in conversation?

The thrust of the book has been about conversations with different people. Individuals might be asked to reflect finally on the extent to which conversations with God are similar or different to conversations with other individuals.

Key Bible passages

Listening conversations
Jesus as a boy with the teachers   Lk. 2.41–52
Jesus on the road to Emmaus   Lk. 24.13–35

Encouraging conversations
Jesus talks with the woman at the well   Jn 4.1–26
Jesus talks to the disciples   Jn 14.1–14

Challenging conversations
Jesus and Nicodemus   Jn 3.1–16
Jesus questioned by the Pharisees   Mk 2.23–3.6

Short conversations
Jesus and Zacchaeus   Lk. 19.1–10
Jesus and the blind man   Mk 8.22–26

Painful conversations
Jesus and the rich young ruler   Mk 10.17–31
Jesus in Gethsemane   Mk 14.32–42

Unresponsive conversations
Jesus and Judas   Lk. 22.47–53
Jesus on the cross   Mk 15.33–39

Joyful conversations
Jesus and Peter   Jn 13.1–17
Jesus with Mary and then the disciples   Jn 20.10–23

Bibliography

Adam, D. (1989), *Tides and Seasons*, London: SPCK.

Allan, D. Kingdom, M., Murrin, K. and Rudkin, D. (1999), *What If: how to start a creative revolution*, London: Capstone.

Bibb, S. and Kourdi, J. (2004), *Trust Matters: for organisational and personal success*, London: Palgrave.

Bonhoeffer, D. (1954), *Life Together*, New York: Harper and Row.

Dickson, A, (2004), *Difficult Conversations*, London: Judy Piatkus.

Dollard, K., Marett-Crosby, A. and Wright, T. (2002), *Doing Business with Benedict*, London: Continuum.

Erickson, J. (2004), *The Art of Persuasion*, London: Hodder and Stoughton.

Kitchen, M. (2003), *A Talent for Living: reflecting on faith and its fruits*, London: SPCK.

Knight, K. (2004), 'Modern Times', London: *Daily Mail* (23 December).

Lindahl, K. (2002), *The Sacred Art of Listening*, Glasgow: Wild Goose Publications.

Long, A. (1990), *Listening*, London: Darton, Longman and Todd.

Mandela, N. (1994), *Long Walk to Freedom*, Cape Town: Abacus.

Mitton, M. (2004), *A Heart to Listen*, Oxford: Bible Reading Fellowship.

Bibliography

Montefiore, H. (1995), *Oh God, What Next*, London: Hodder and Stoughton.

Nouwen, H. J. M. (1976), *Reaching Out*, London: Fount.

Pease, A. and B. (2004), *The Definitive Book of Body Language*, London: Orion.

Pinsent, M. (2004), 'Partridge trains sights on golden road ahead', London: *The Times* (4 December).

Rumbelow, H. (2004), 'Where the streets have no shame', London: *The Times* (4 December).

Sacks, J, (2000), *Celebrating Life*, London: Continuum.

Sacks, J. (2002), *The Dignity of Difference*, London: Continuum.

Sachs, J. (2002), 'Listening is the greatest gift we can give a troubled soul', *The Times* (14 December).

Schulter, M. (2004), 'Relational Apologetics', article in Issue 8 of *Engage*, London: Jubilee Centre.

Shaw, Patricia (2002), *Changing Conversations in Organisations: a complexity approach to change*, London: Routledge.

Shaw, Peter (2004), *Mirroring Jesus as Leader*, Cambridge: Grove.

Stone, D., Patton, B. and Heen, S. (2000), *Difficult Conversations*, London: Penguin.

Trent Hughes, J. (2004), *Tough Talk Made Easy*, London: Element.

Wheatley, M. J. (2002), *Turning to One Another: simple conversations to restore hope in the future*, San Francisco: Berrett-Koehler.